DECORATIV
CROSS STITCH

DECORATIVE
CROSS STITCH

Over 40 delightful designs for decorating items in your home

Maria Diaz

NEW HOLLAND

First published in 2003 by
New Holland Publishers (UK) Ltd
London · Cape Town · Sydney · Auckland

Garfield House, 86–88 Edgware Road
London W2 2EA
United Kingdom
www.newhollandpublishers.com

80 McKenzie Street
Cape Town 8001
South Africa

Level 1, Unit 4, 14 Aquatic Drive
Frenchs Forest, NSW 2086
Australia

218 Lake Road
Northcote, Auckland
New Zealand

ISBN 1 84330 684 0

Senior Editor: **Clare Sayer**
Production: **Hazel Kirkman**
Design: **Lisa Tai**
Photographer: **Shona Wood**
Illustrators: **Stephen Dew** and **Kate Simunek**
Editorial Direction: **Rosemary Wilkinson**

10 9 8 7 6 5 4 3 2

Reproduction by Modern Age Repro, Hong Kong
Printed and bound by Times Offset (M) Sdn Bhd, Malaysia

Special thanks to the following for stitching the finished projects:
Jane Chamberlain, Michaela Learner, Angela Ottewell,
Christine Thompson.

Contents

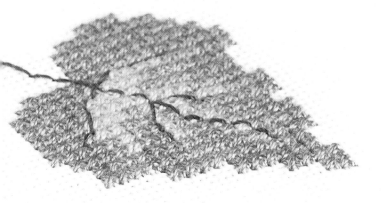

Introduction	6
Materials and techniques	8

Fruit and Flower Motifs — 12

Summer fruits	14
Art Deco rose sewing set	18
Red poppies	22
Green leaves table linen	26
Daisy picnic basket	30
Camellia bed linen	34

Picture Motifs — 38

Seashell bathroom	40
Windmill pantry	44
Green linen teaset	48
Gingham playmat and pram toys	52
Architectural drawing	56
Japanese lady	60

Animal Motifs — 64

Farmyard animals	66
Cute cats breakfast set	70
Teddy Bear baby set	74
Blue bird bed linen	78
Seaside bathroom	82

Geometric Motifs — 86

Blue and white sampler	88
Playing card motifs	92
Red and white table linen	96
Turkish bathroom	100

DMC chart	104
Anchor conversion chart	110
Suppliers	111
Index	112

Introduction

Cross stitch first appeared in the sixteenth century and was traditionally used in samplers. Although samplers are now a design practice in their own right, they were first used as a reference for stitches and patterns and as a means for young embroiderers to practise their skills.

Once you have mastered the basic stitch, working with cross stitch is a wonderful way to create pictures. From really simple silhouettes to intricate flower studies, the technique is the same. If you can read a pattern then you will be able to tackle the most elaborate designs with confidence. In this book I have included a wide range of motifs to appeal to all tastes and skill levels, illustrating how versatile cross stitch can be.

Coming from a fine art background, I like to challenge the way cross stitch is perceived. As well as creating pictures, it is fun to come up with different ways in which to exhibit your stitching because if you become a fanatic, as many do, you will soon run out of wall space. From picnic baskets to address books, I enjoy adding little personal touches with cross stitch. Within this book I have tried to show how easy it is to use your embroidery in more imaginative ways around the home. It doesn't have to be all doilies and antimacassars you know.

Materials and techniques

Cross stitch is a simple stitch usually worked on evenweave linens or Aida (a specialist blockweave). The stitch itself is formed by two diagonal stitches, one lying diagonally over the other to create a cross. The stitches can be worked individually or 'row by row', working a row of diagonal stitches (or half cross stitch) in one direction and then stitching back over them in the opposite direction to form the crosses. The following pages will provide you with all the information you need on materials, techniques and caring for your finished items. All the materials and equipment used in this book can be easily obtained from good needlework or craft shops (see page 111 for more details).

FABRICS

Cross stitch is generally worked on evenweave fabrics such as Aida, hardanger, specialist evenweaves and linens. Evenweave means that the same number of threads are counted in both directions over 2.5 cm (1 in). It is sometimes referred to as 14-, 18- or 28-count. Aida is a specially designed fabric where the fabric threads are set into blocks giving a grid-like appearance and creating definite holes. Hardanger has its threads woven in pairs, again making it easy to see the holes. The specialist evenweaves and linens are loosely woven so you can count the threads and slip your needle through with ease.

When working on evenweave linen, it is usual to stitch over two of the fabric threads, which will essentially halve the fabric count, so a 28-count linen will only give you 14 stitches to the inch. It is important to remember this when working out design sizes.

Fabric counts are usually calculated in inches, to work out the finished size of a pattern simply divide the number of stitches by the fabric count and that will give you a pretty accurate design size in inches. For example a motif, 40 stitches square, when worked on a 14-count fabric, will measure approximately 7.5 cm (3 in) square, but on an 18-count it will be only 6 cm (2¼ in).

THREADS

Stranded cotton is probably the most widely used embroidery thread on the market and comes as a 6-stranded length. You have to separate the threads one by one and then lay them back together in the quantities required. The number of strands required will vary depending on the fabric count; the chart below can be used as a guide.

Fabric count	Needle size	No. of stranded cotton strands
8-count	22	6 – cross stitch 2 – backstitch
11-count	24	3 – cross stitch 1 – backstitch
14-count, 16-count	26	2 – cross stitch 1 – backstitch
18-count 22-count	26	1 – cross stitch 1 – backstitch

NEEDLES

Tapestry needles are most often used when working cross stitch as they have a large eye and blunt end, which are easily pushed through the natural holes of the fabric.

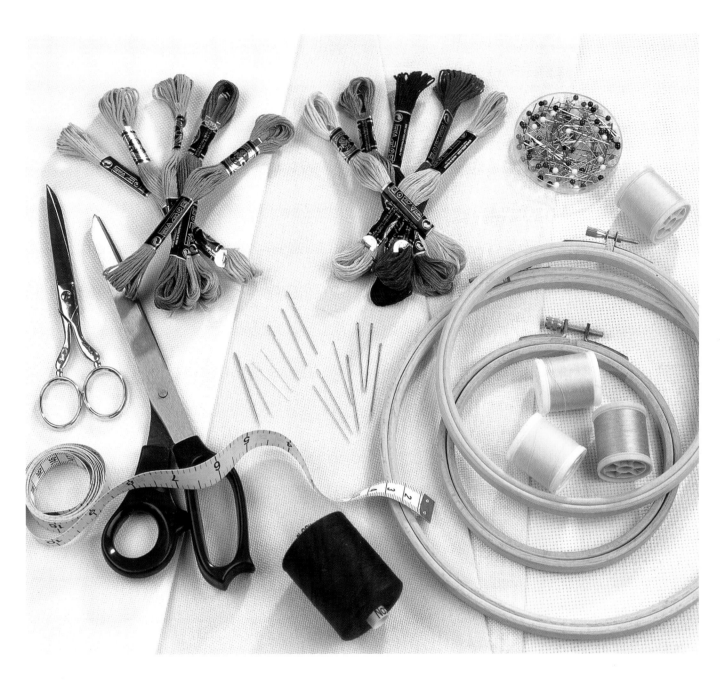

Chenille needles have a larger eye than embroidery needles and are the best ones to use when working with waste canvas.

You need to choose an appropriate sized needle, which will depend on the thread and fabric used; the chart opposite can be used as a guide.

CHARTS

Cross stitch charts are easy to read, each square on the pattern represents one stitch. Quarter and three-quarter stitches are used only when a square is divided diagonally in half and has a tiny symbol in one or both sections. Backstitch is usually shown as a bold line.

Above: Cross stitch fabrics, stranded cottons and needles are the only essential materials you need to do a cross stitch project, but the following items are also useful: embroidery scissors, dressmaking scissors, tape measure, tacking thread, sewing thread and pins, as well as embroidery hoops to keep the fabric taut while you work.

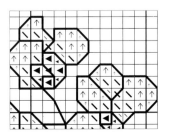

Left: This chart is a detail of the smaller chart on page 62. In this case, the small arrow symbol taking up just half of one square represents a quarter stitch. The bold lines indicate where backstitch is required.

EMBROIDERY HOOPS AND FRAMES

Embroidery hoops and frames come in a wide range of sizes from tiny 8 cm (3 in) hoops for small motifs to large freestanding frames for heirloom projects. It is always best wherever possible to use a frame or hoop. They are designed to keep the fabric taut whilst stitching, which in turn helps to regulate the tension of your sewing and keep the stitches even. Do not stretch the fabric too tightly in the hoop and remove the hoop when not stitching to prevent permanent distortions to your stitches or fabric.

ADDITIONAL EQUIPMENT

There are a few other essentials you will need to have to hand. Dressmaking scissors for cutting your fabric, embroidery scissors for trimming threads and contrasting tacking thread to indicate centre marks and guide lines. For making up your projects you will need a basic sewing kit (tape measure, pins, sewing thread, needles, scissors), sewing machine and additional fabrics and trimmings, which will be individually listed for each project.

AFTER CARE

When you have finished a project it can look a little creased and grubby, so knowing how to clean the materials used is important. Most threads on the market today are colourfast but do read the manufacturer's instructions before washing anything. If you are choosing a thread for an item which will require regular cleaning, ensure that it is colourfast or the time you spend sewing could be longer than the life of that item!

Depending on the fabric used, virtually all your work can be hand washed carefully in warm water using a mild detergent. It is even possible to use your washing machine on a delicate cycle as long as the fabric edges are finished properly and all stray threads are firmly secured.

Once washed it is best to press the stitching whilst still damp, as ironing will restore the stiffness lost during sewing. Place the stitched piece face down on to a towel to prevent the stitches being flattened. Using a cool iron, press carefully.

GETTING STARTED

When working a counted cross stitch design it is always best (unless otherwise instructed) to start stitching from the centre of the pattern and work outward. This will ensure the motif's correct position on the fabric. Cross stitch patterns usually have the centres indicated. The easiest way to find the fabric centre is as follows: fold the fabric in half vertically then horizontally and press firmly on the folds to create definite creases. When the fabric is laid out flat again it will be divided into quarters. Using a contrasting colour to the fabric, work a line of tacking along each crease – where they cross is the centre of the fabric piece.

A good tip is to overestimate your fabric size leaving yourself a couple of extra centimetres all the way round. This enables you to secure your edges and leaves you room for mistakes (if you didn't quite start in the centre or forgot to allow for wording around the design etc.). It is also a good idea to secure the fabric edges to prevent fraying. This can be achieved by either binding, over-sewing or zig-zagging with a sewing machine.

STARTING AND FINISHING

Working from the front, push the needle through about 4 cm (1½ in) to one side, bringing it back through where you intend to begin. Start stitching the first line, making sure you catch in the thread at the back. Once it is secure pull the loose end through. If this proves difficult simply pull the end through to the back when you have finished stitching. Thread it through the needle and darn the end under a few stitches to secure. This is also the best way to finish off – it is important not to use knots as they create lumps and may eventually work loose or snag.

Individual cross stitch

Looking at the stitch as a square, bring the needle out in the bottom right corner and work a diagonal stitch to top left. Then bring the needle through in the bottom left and cross the first stitch with another diagonal stitch into the top right corner.

Cross stitch, row-by-row

Work a row of diagonal stitches from bottom right to top left. Then work a row of diagonal stitches in the opposite direction crossing the first ones. I work this way as I am right-handed, so I do not drag my hand across the finished stitches. However it is not important which way you work as long as all the top diagonals face the same direction.

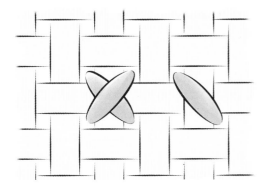

Individual cross stitch and half cross stitch

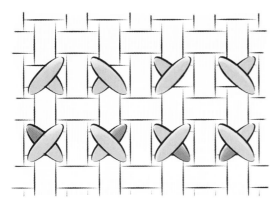

Cross stitch, row-by-row

Quarter and three-quarter stitches

Back stitch

Half cross stitch

Half cross stitch is a single diagonal stitch, which as it states is half a cross stitch. It can be worked from either bottom right to top left, or from bottom left to top right.

Quarter and three-quarter stitches

Quarter and three-quarter stitches fill in half the space of a full cross stitch on the chart. A three-quarter stitch is worked by stitching one diagonal (or half cross stitch) and then instead of working the crossing stitch from corner to corner pass it through the centre of the stitch. A quarter stitch is simply half of a diagonal (or half cross stitch) worked from corner to middle.

Back stitch

Work a single straight stitch, then bring the needle out a stitch length ahead and then back to link up the line. Backstitch can be worked in any direction and is used to outline designs and add detail.

French knots

French knots are great for adding texture and work well within cross stitch designs. Holding the thread taut wrap it twice around the needle. Then still holding the thread taut insert the needle back into the fabric close to where it emerged and pull the thread through.

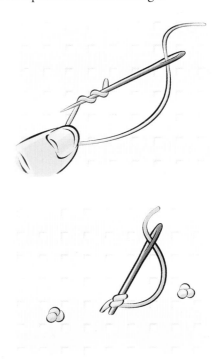

French knots

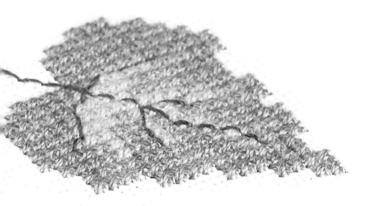

Fruit and Flower Motifs

We often look to nature and wonder at her beauty and elegance. Here we have a taste of how that charm can be portrayed in cross stitch. From simple daisy motifs dancing along a picnic cloth to intricate flower studies, this chapter has something for every skill level.

Summer fruits

Brighten up your kitchen with some luscious red fruits or label your preserve pots with specific motifs. These fruit motifs are simple but effective and can be stitched on to all manner of items — not just items for the home. These fun kitchen accessories are the perfect thing for the organic gardener.

SKILL LEVEL: 1

MEASUREMENTS

When worked on 14-count Aida with each cross stitch worked over one fabric block, the strawberry motif for the jam pot cover measures 3 x 4 cm (1 x 1½ in). The strawberry and cherry motif (which is repeated along the band) measures 10 x 3 cm (4 x 1 in).

YOU WILL NEED
For the embroidery
- 20 cm (8 in) 14-count white Aida
- 5 cm (2 in) Aida band (tea towel width)
- Tapestry needle, size 26
- Embroidery hoop
- Scissors
- Contrasting tacking thread
- Soft pencil
- DMC stranded cottons as listed

To make up the projects
- Basic sewing kit
- Sewing machine
- Matching sewing thread
- Bias binding
- Plain tea towel

Colour		Shade	No. of skeins
	red	350	1
	peach	351	1
	bright green	702	1
	lime green	704	1
	brown	779	1
	blue	798	1
	dark red	817	1
	light green	913	1
	pale mint	955	1
	white	blanc	1

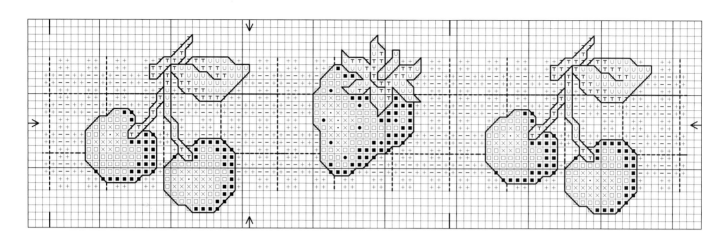

Symbol	Colour	Backstitch	Shade
▢	red		350
✕	peach		351
T	bright green		702
U	lime green		704
	brown	◩	779
	blue	◪	798
◼	dark red		817
−	light green		913
+	pale mint		955
·	white		blanc

Above: A strawberry motif on a jam pot cover.

Right: Repeat the design along the Aida band to fit your item.

TEA TOWEL BAND

1 To calculate the amount of Aida band required, measure the width of your tea towel and add 2 cm (1 in).

2 Fold the band in half and mark the centre with tacking. Then fold lengthways to find the horizontal centre and tack another short line, where the lines cross marks the centre and starting point.

3 Using two strands of cotton for cross stitch and one for backstitch, work the design shown on the chart opposite.

4 Repeat the design along the band leaving a 4 cm (1½ in) gap at either end. [Repeat marks are indicated as short black lines on the chart.]

5 Remove the tacking and gently press with a cool iron. Position the Aida band on the tea towel, pin and tack in place. Machine or slip stitch in place remembering to turn under the end of the band to keep it neat.

JAM POT COVER

1 Cut a 20 cm (8 in) square of 14-count white Aida and bind the edges using coloured bias binding.

2 Mark the centre of the fabric with tacking. With a soft pencil indicate on the chart the centre of a single fruit.

3 Using two strands of cotton for cross stitch and one for backstitch, stitch the motif from the centre out.

4 When complete remove the tacking and press with a cool iron.

Art Deco rose sewing set

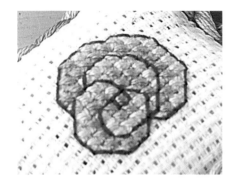

These stylish Art Deco Rose accessories would be a delightful addition to any needlework enthusiast's sewing box. In clear yet subtle shades, the simple symmetry reflects the chic elegance of the Deco era. A pretty pin cushion, needle case and scissor fob mean that you will always have your essential sewing kit to hand.

SKILL LEVEL: 1

MEASUREMENTS

Worked on 14-count Aida and with each cross stitch worked over one fabric block, the scissor fob motif measures 2 x 2 cm (1 x 1 in), the needle case motif measures 4 x 6 cm (1½ x 2½ in) and the pin cushion measures 9 x 9 cm (4 x 4 in).

YOU WILL NEED

For the embroidery
- 14 cm (5 in) square, white 14-count Aida
- 17 x 11 cm (6½ x 4 in) white 14-count Aida
- 6 cm (2½ in) square, white 14-count Aida
- Tapestry needle, size 26
- Embroidery hoop
- Scissors
- Contrasting tacking thread
- DMC stranded cottons as listed

To make up the projects
- Basic sewing kit
- Sewing machine
- Pinking shears
- Polyester stuffing
- 25 x 11 cm (10 x 4 in) piece of felt
- 25 cm (10 in) square backing fabric
- 1 m (3 ft) coordinating cord

Colour		Shade	No. of skeins
■	emerald green	562	1
□	pale green	563	1
■	burgundy	902	1
■	dusky pink	3687	1
□	light pink	3688	1

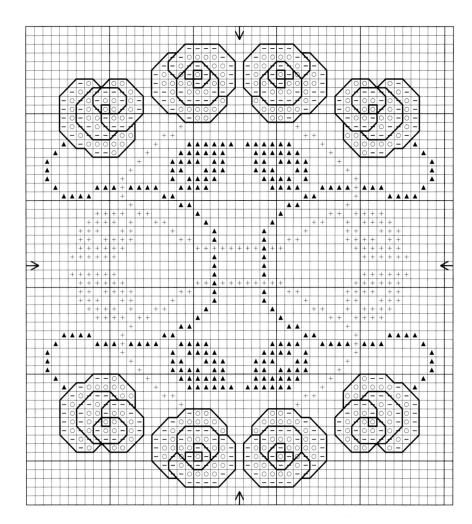

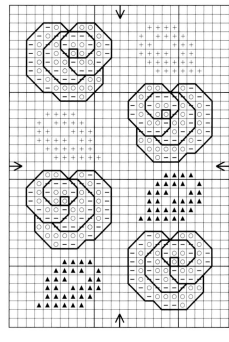

◁ Chart A　　　　　　　　　△ Chart B

Symbol	Colour	Backstitch	Shade
▲	emerald green		562
+	pale green		563
	burgundy	◺	902
○	dusky pink		3687
−	light pink		3688

PIN CUSHION

1 Mark the centre of a 14 cm (5 in) square of Aida with tacking.

2 Using two strands of stranded cotton for cross-stitch and one for backstitch work the pin cushion design (chart A) from the centre out over one fabric block.

3 When you have completed the stitching remove the tacking and gently press on the reverse with a cool iron.

4 Cut backing fabric into a 14 cm (5 in) square. Lay the backing fabric and stitched piece together, right sides facing, pin and tack in place.

5 With a 1 cm (½ in) seam allowance stitch together, leaving a 6 cm (2½ in) gap in one side to turn through.

6 Remove tacking and turn right side out, gently pushing out the corners. Fill the cushion with polyester stuffing and slipstitch the gap shut.

7 Finally using slipstitch again in a matching colour, attach a coordinating cord around the edge leaving a loop at one corner.

SCISSOR FOB

1 Take a 6 cm (2½ in) square of Aida and mark the centre with tacking.
2 Using two strands for cross stitch and one for backstitch, stitch a single rose motif from the centre out over one fabric block.
3 When you have completed the stitching, remove the tacking and gently press.

Above: Choose a cord in a coordinating colour to trim the pin cushion.

4 Cut backing fabric to a 6 cm (2½ in) square and follow steps 4–6 for the pin cushion above to make up the tiny cushion.
5 When the cushion is finished, stitch a cord all the way round with a 7 cm (3 in) long loop to one corner so it can be attached to your scissors.

NEEDLE CASE

1 Cut a 17 x 11 cm (6½ x 4 in) piece of Aida. Fold the fabric in half widthways, marking out the centre of the right half with tacking. Stitch the needle case design (chart B) from the centre of this half. Using two strands for cross stitch and one for backstitch, work over one fabric block. Remove tacking and press.
2 Trim the Aida eight blocks from the design along the top, bottom and right hand side and 9 cm (3½ in) from the left of the design.
3 Fray the fabric on all four sides by carefully pulling out two blocks of threads.
4 Measure the finished size of the design and using pinking shears cut a piece of felt 1 cm (½ in) larger all round. Again using pinking shears, cut another piece of felt half the size of the first.
5 With the stitching face down, place the largest piece of felt over the top, then position the smaller piece in the centre on top of that.
6 Pin, then stitch all three layers together in one line down the centre and fold in half to form a book.

Red poppies

Bring a touch of the autumn harvest into your home with this stunning poppy picture and matching cushion. Modern and stylish, this rich red flower study is given a hint of rustic charm when stitched on to natural linen and made up into a bench cushion with chunky wooden buttons.

SKILL LEVEL: 2

MEASUREMENTS

Worked on 32-count linen with each cross stitch worked over three fabric threads, the picture motif measures 21 x 12 cm (8½ x 4½ in). With each stitch worked over two fabric threads, the cushion motif measures 14 x 8 cm (5½ x 3 in).

YOU WILL NEED

For the embroidery
- 40 x 30 cm (16 x 12 in), 32-count white Belfast linen
- 44 x 26 cm (17¼ x 20½ in), 32-count natural Belfast linen
- Tapestry needle, size 26
- Tapestry needle, size 24
- Embroidery hoop
- Scissors
- Contrasting tacking thread
- DMC stranded cottons as listed

To make up the projects
- Basic sewing kit
- Sewing machine
- White sewing thread
- 4 x large wooden buttons
- 88 x 54 cm (34¾ x 21¼ in), white linen
- 60 x 40 cm (23½ x 16 in) cushion pad

Colour	Shade	No. of skeins
burnt rose	221	1
black	310	1
dark green	319	1
coral	350	1
peach	352	1
apple	471	1
red	817	1
grass green	989	1
pale green	3348	1
forest green	3363	1
green	3364	1
tangerine	3825	1

PICTURE

1 Fold the 40 x 30 cm (16 x 12 in) piece of white 32-count linen in half horizontally and vertically. With contrasting cotton stitch a line of tacking along each crease. This marks the fabric centre.

2 With a size 24 needle, begin stitching from the centre out using three strands for cross stitch and French knots and two for the backstitch. Work each stitch over three fabric threads.

3 When all the stitching has been completed, remove the tacking and press.

4 Either frame the design yourself or take to a professional.

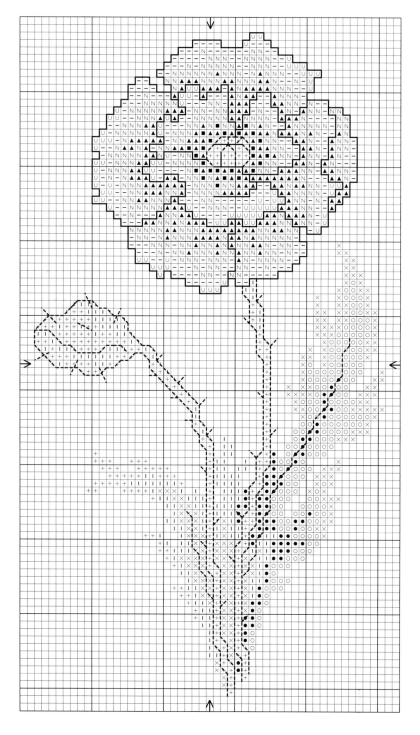

Symbol	Colour	Backstitch	Shade
	burnt rose	◥	2211
	dark green	◥	319
N	coral		350
−	peach		352
I	apple		471
▲	red		817
✕	grass green		989
+	pale green		3348
●	forest green		3363
O	green		3364
U	tangerine		3825

Symbol	Colour	French knot	Shade
	black	■	310

Right: Worked over three fabric threads the poppy motif is larger.

CUSHION COVER

1 Cut your piece of natural linen in half so you have two 44 x 26 cm (17¼ x 10¼ in) pieces. Mark the centre of one piece with tacking.

2 With a size 26 needle, begin stitching using two strands for cross stitch and French knots and one for the backstitch. Work each stitch over two fabric threads. When complete remove the tacking and press.

3 Cut your piece of white linen in half so you have two 44 x 54 cm (17¼ x 21¼ in) pieces.

4 Lay the stitched piece and one white piece right sides together and taking a 3 cm (1¼ in) seam allowance, stitch their right-hand edges together. Repeat with the other two pieces.

5 Zig-zag or over sew the edges to prevent fraying and press the seams open.

6 Fold over 4 cm (1½ in) then 6 cm (2¼ in) at the opposite end to the natural linen on each piece (see diagram A). Pin and tack in place. These now make up the front and back of your cushion.

7 On the front cushion panel (the one with the stitching) stitch four buttonholes that are 8 cm (3¼ in) apart.

8 Place the two panels right sides together and taking a 3 cm (1¼ in) seam allowance, stitch three sides together leaving the end with the button holes open (see diagram B).

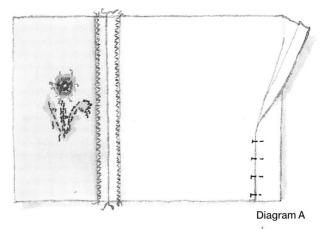

Diagram A

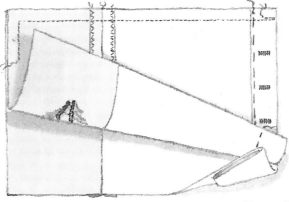

Diagram B

9 Remove all the tacking and zig-zag or over sew the edges to prevent fraying. Turn right side out and press, then stitch the four buttons in place and put in your cushion pad.

Left: The cushion motif is smaller when stitched over two fabric threads.

Green leaves table linen

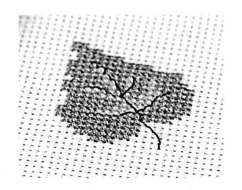

Bring a touch of the outdoors into your dining room with these wonderful fresh green leaves. They are the perfect motifs to add a hint of nature to your table linen. Scatter them across a tablecloth or use single motifs to bring a touch of style to napkins and accessories.

SKILL LEVEL: 2

MEASUREMENTS
Worked on the Bornholm tablecloth the largest leaf motif measures 4.5 x 5 cm (1¾ x 2 in). The napkin motif measures 3.5 x 3.5 cm (1½ x 1½ in).

NOTE
Measurements and quantities given are for one tablecloth, two napkins and two coasters.

YOU WILL NEED
For the embroidery
• E1310, Bornholm table cloth
• 60 x 60 cm (24 x 24 in) 28-count evenweave linen
• Tapestry needle, size 26
• Embroidery hoop
• Scissors
• Contrasting tacking thread
• White sewing thread
• DMC stranded cottons as listed

To make up the projects
• Basic sewing kit
• Sewing machine
• Acrylic coaster

	Colour	Shade	No. of skeins
	dusky green	320	1
	light green	368	1
	pale mint	369	1
	apple green	471	1
	lime green	472	1
	bright green	989	2
	dark green	3362	1
	forest green	3363	1
	leaf green	3364	1

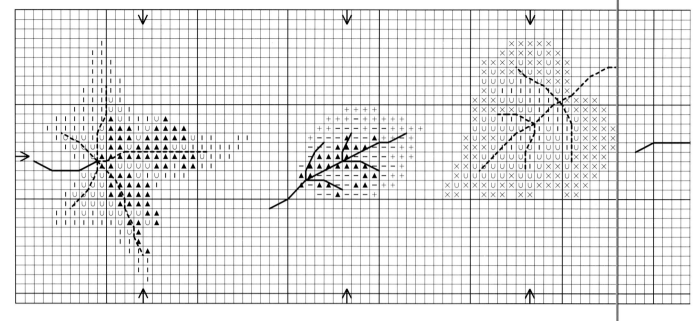

Symbol	Colour	Backstitch	Shade
▲	dusky green		320
−	light green		368
+	pale mint		369
U	apple green		471
I	lime green	◺	472
×	bright green		989
■	dark green	◿	3362
●	forest green		3363
○	leaf green		3364

Above: Choose one of the leaves to stitch on to a napkin.

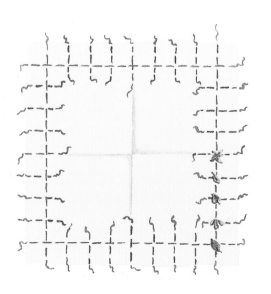

Left: The diagram shows where you should position the leaves along the edges of the tablecloth.

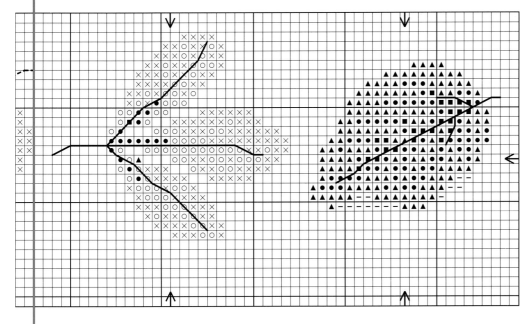

◁ overlap pattern from this point

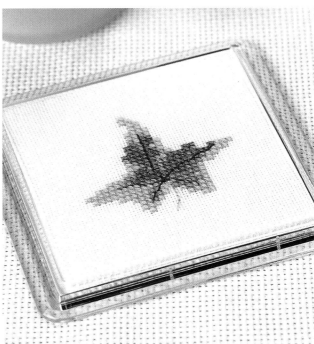

Below: The acrylic coaster keeps the motif in pristine condition.

TABLE CLOTH

1 Stitch a line of tacking 17 blocks in from the panel edge on all four sides. Fold the cloth in half vertically and horizontally and stitch a short line of tacking down each crease crossing the tacked square. This will mark the central point of each side.

2 Stitch three short lines either side of the centre line at equal intervals between the central point and the tacked corner (see diagram opposite). This will give you 32 intersections, marking the centre of each leaf to be stitched.

3 Using two strands of cotton for cross stitch and one for backstitch, work each stitch over one fabric block. Start from the central point on one side and work the first leaf from the centre out, then following the chart, stitch each leaf in sequence from left to right. Then stitch the leaves in reverse order to the left, omitting the last leaf.

4 Once you have completed the first side, turn the cloth 90° and stitch the next quarter, continue like this until all four quarters are finished. Remove the tacking and gently press with a cool iron.

NAPKIN

1 Hem a 30 cm (12 in) square of evenweave linen by folding over 1 cm (⅜ in) then 1.5 cm (½ in) and machine stitch in place.

2 Then, in one corner, tack two short lines running parallel with the edges approximately 10 cm (4 in) in from the hemmed edge. Using where they cross as the central mark, stitch a single leaf.

3 Use two strands of cotton for cross stitch and one for backstitch, work each stitch over two fabric threads. Remove the tacking and gently press with a cool iron.

COASTER

1 Cut a piece of evenweave linen 15 cm (6 in) square.

2 Mark the centre and stitch a single leaf using two strands of cotton for cross stitch and one for backstitch. Work each stitch over two fabric threads.

3 When complete back with Vilene and make up the coaster using supplier's instructions.

Daisy picnic basket

Why not add a hint of nostalgia to your summer day trips by dressing up an old basket to carry all your picnic treats in? These delicate white daisies look pretty, yet modern when stitched on to rich blue linen, making these the perfect accessories for a lazy summer picnic.

SKILL LEVEL: 2

MEASUREMENTS
Worked on 32-count linen with each cross stitch worked over two fabric threads, the tablecloth motif (which is repeated to make a border) measures 10 x 6 cm (4 x 2½ in). A single daisy motif measures 5 x 5 cm (2 x 2 in).

YOU WILL NEED
For the embroidery
- 60 cm (24 in) 32-count regal blue, Belfast linen
- Tapestry needle, size 26
- Embroidery hoop
- Scissors
- Contrasting tacking thread
- Matching sewing thread
- DMC stranded cottons as listed

To make up the projects
- Basic sewing kit
- Sewing machine
- 1.8 m (6 ft) coordinating fabric
- 2 m (6½ ft) 3 cm (1¼ in) wide coordinating ribbon
- 40 cm (15½ in) medium weight wadding
- Brown paper and pencil
- Basket

Colour		Shade	No. of skeins
	light green	164	2
	light sand	676	1
	dark sand	729	1
	palest pink	819	1
	light pink	963	2
	grass green	988	1
	silver plum	3042	1
	white	blanc	2

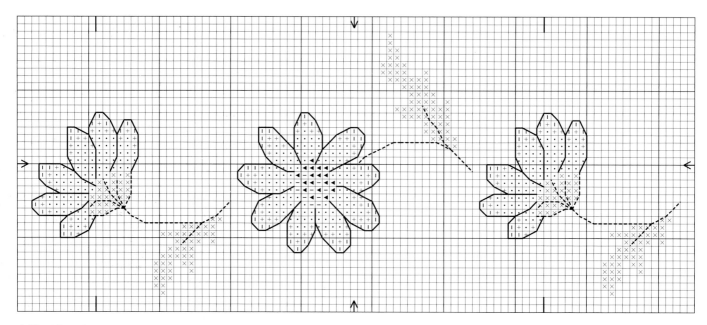

△ Chart A

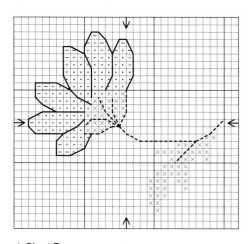

△ Chart B

Symbol	Colour	Backstitch	Shade
☒	light green		164
Ⅰ	light sand		676
▲	dark sand		729
⊞	palest pink		819
⊟	light pink		963
	grass green	◰	988
	silver plum	◳	3042
⊡	white		blanc

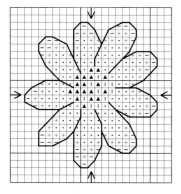

△ Chart C

Right: The daisy motif is repeated to fit the length of the tablecloth.

PICNIC CLOTH

1 Cut a strip of linen 21 cm (8¼ in) wide (fabric is supplied in 140 cm/55 in widths) and mark the fabric centre with tacking.

2 Using two strands of stranded cotton for cross stitch and one for backstitch, work each stitch over two fabric threads. Start stitching from the centre out (see chart A).

3 Using the repeat marks as a guide (indicated in bold lines on the chart) continue stitching the daisies along the whole length of the fabric. Finish with a complete flower at least 10 cm (4 in) from either end.

4 Once you have completed the stitching remove the tacking thread and press gently with a cool iron on the wrong side.

5 Taking a 3 cm (1¼ in) hem allowance and with the right sides facing, attach the embroidered piece down the length of a coordinating piece of fabric 140 x 120 cm (55 x 47¼ in) to form your picnic cloth.

6 Press open the seam and zig-zag or overstitch the edges to prevent fraying. Finally hem the whole cloth, turning over 2 cm (¾ in) then 3 cm (1¼ in).

PICNIC BASKET

1 Use the brown paper to make a pattern for the basket lid. Place the paper over the basket and notch out a space for the handles. Trim round the shape leaving about a 3 cm (1¼ in) overhang.

2 Using this pattern, cut a piece of linen, coordinating fabric and wadding to shape.

3 Randomly stitch a selection of daisies across the linen making sure the motifs are at least 10 cm (4 in) in from the edges (charts B and C). Once you have completed the stitching, press gently with a cool iron on the wrong side of the stitching.

Above: Single daisies are stitched randomly on to the basket cover.

4 Taking the piece of coordinating fabric, pin then tack the ribbon all the way round the edge. Cut the remaining ribbon into four equal lengths and tack to either side of the handle area (see diagram A).

5 Lay the embroidered and coordinating fabric pieces together with the ribbon and the cross stitch on the inside. Place the wadding on top and pin, then tack the three layers together (see diagram B).

6 Taking a 1.5 cm (½ in) seam allowance, stitch the layers together leaving a 20 cm (8 in) gap to turn through.

7 When you have stitched all three layers securely together turn right side out and slip stitch the gap shut.

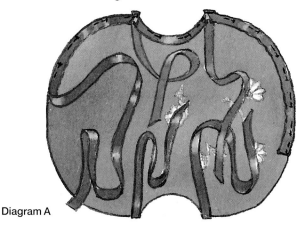

Diagram A

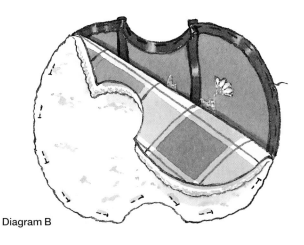

Diagram B

Camellia bed linen

This pretty pink camellia design is the perfect motif for beautiful bed linen. Depending on what size it is used at, the motif has different effects: 10-count waste canvas is used to make a bold statement on the pillowcase but the same motif appears more delicate and precious when stitched on to linen.

SKILL LEVEL: 3

MEASUREMENTS

Worked on 10-count waste canvas, the pillow motif measures 14 x 14 cm (5½ x 5½ in). With each cross stitch worked over one fabric block, the sheet motif measures 8 x 8 cm (3 x 3 in). Worked on 32-count linen with each cross stitch worked over two fabric threads, the trinket box motif measures 8 x 8 cm (3 x 3 in).

NOTE

Measurements and quantities given are for a single sheet. Double the number of motifs and thread quantities for a double or king sized sheet.

YOU WILL NEED

For the embroidery
- 18 cm (7 in) square of 10-count waste canvas
- 14 cm (5½ in) white Aida band (sheet width)
- 18 x 18 cm (7 x 7 in) white 32-count linen
- Tapestry needle, size 26
- Chenille needle, size 24
- Embroidery hoop
- Scissors
- Contrasting tacking thread
- DMC stranded cottons as listed

To make up the projects
- Basic sewing kit
- Sewing machine
- White sewing thread
- Tweezers
- Trinket box

Colour	Shade	No. of skeins
darkest green	500	1
mid sand	676	1
light sand	677	1
dark sand	729	1
palest pink	819	2
soft pink	963	2
forest green	987	1
fresh green	988	2
light green	989	1
warm pink	3716	2
dark terracotta	3721	1
white	blanc	2

Symbol	Colour	Backstitch	Shade
	darkest green	◪	500
○	mid sand		676
−	light sand		677
Z	dark sand		729
+	palest pink		819
I	soft pink		963
▲	forest green		987
□	fresh green		988
⊠	light green		989
●	warm pink		3716
	dark terracotta	◻	3721
·	white		blanc

SHEET BAND

1 To calculate the amount of Aida band required, measure the width of your sheet and add 5 cm (2 in).

2 Fold the band in half and mark the centre with a line of tacking. Stitch two further lines at 25 cm (10 in) intervals to either side. Then fold lengthways to find the horizontal centre and tack a series of short lines crossing the first ones. Where the lines cross marks the centre and starting point of each motif.

3 Using two lengths of stranded cotton for cross stitch and one for backstitch, work each stitch over one fabric block.

4 When you have completed all the motifs remove the tacking and using a cool iron press the band gently from the wrong side.

5 Pin and tack the Aida band about 8 cm (3 in) from the top of the sheet, with the design upside down so that when the sheet is turned over it will read the right way.

6 Either machine or slip stitch in place remembering to turn in the untidy end of the band to keep it neat.

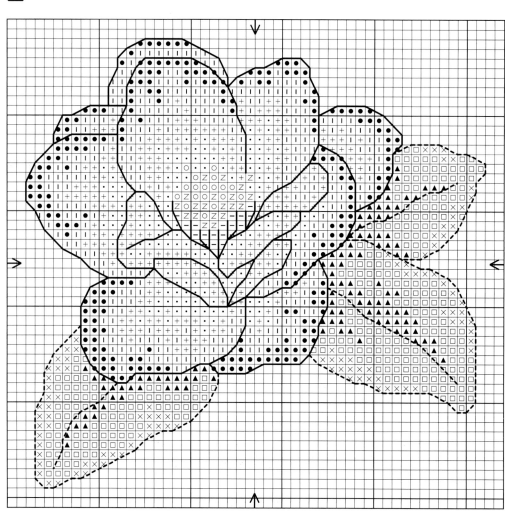

Left: The motifs are stitched on to Aida band and then attached to a sheet.

PILLOW CASES

1 Cut an 18 cm (7 in) square of waste canvas and mark the centre with tacking.

2 Position the canvas on the pillowcase where you want your camellia motif to be and tack into place, remembering to stitch through only one layer.

3 With an embroidery hoop to keep the canvas and pillowcase layer taut, stitch the motif, using the chenille needle. Use four strands for cross stitch and two for backstitch.

4 When the motif has been completed remove all the tacking and damp down the waste canvas. Pull the canvas threads out one at a time using tweezers, then gently press using a cool iron.

TRINKET BOX

1 Cut an 18 cm (7 in) square of linen and mark the centre.

2 Using two lengths of stranded cotton for cross stitch and one for backstitch, work each stitch over two fabric threads.

3 Remove the tacking and press. Make up the trinket box lid using the supplier's instructions.

Left: A matching trinket box completes the bedroom set.

Picture Motifs

The reflective qualities of many of the threads used can give pictures and motifs a wonderful sense of texture and depth by manipulating the shades and colours as one would with painting or drawing. The projects illustrate the different styles you can achieve using the same stitch.

Seashell bathroom

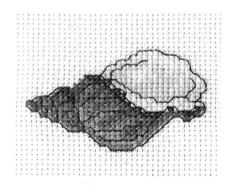

These pretty pink shells are the perfect thing to add some seashore charm to your bathroom. Stitch up a few shells and then frame them to make a sweet little picture or take just one shell motif and repeat it across a towel for a guest bathroom.

SKILL LEVEL: 1

MEASUREMENTS

The towel motif measures 6.5 x 3.5 cm (2½ x 1½ in). Worked on 18-count Aida with each cross stitch worked over one fabric block, the largest picture motif measures 5 x 3.5 cm (2 x 1½ in).

YOU WILL NEED

For the embroidery
- 18 x 14 cm (7 x 5½ in) white 18-count Aida
- Guest towel with 8 cm (3 in) Aida panel
- Tapestry needle, size 26
- Embroidery hoop
- Scissors
- Contrasting tacking thread
- DMC stranded cottons as listed

To make up the projects
- A frame of your choice

Colour	Shade	No. of skeins
palest pink	819	1
baby pink	963	1
dark pink	3350	1
raspberry	3685	1
rose pink	3731	1
soft rose	3733	1
white	blanc	1

Symbol	Colour	Backstitch	Shade
I	palest pink		819
×	baby pink		963
□	dark pink		3350
■	raspberry	⧅	3685
−	rose pink		3731
○	soft rose		3733
+	white		blanc

▷ Chart A

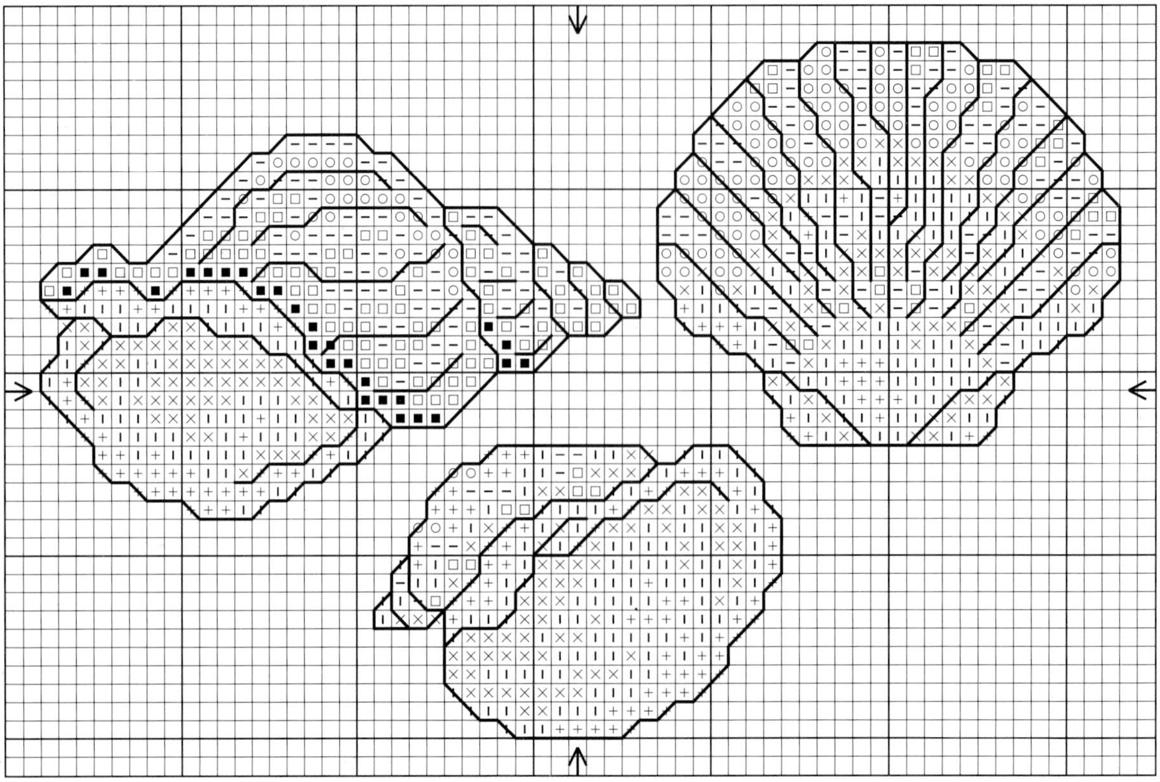

▽ Chart B

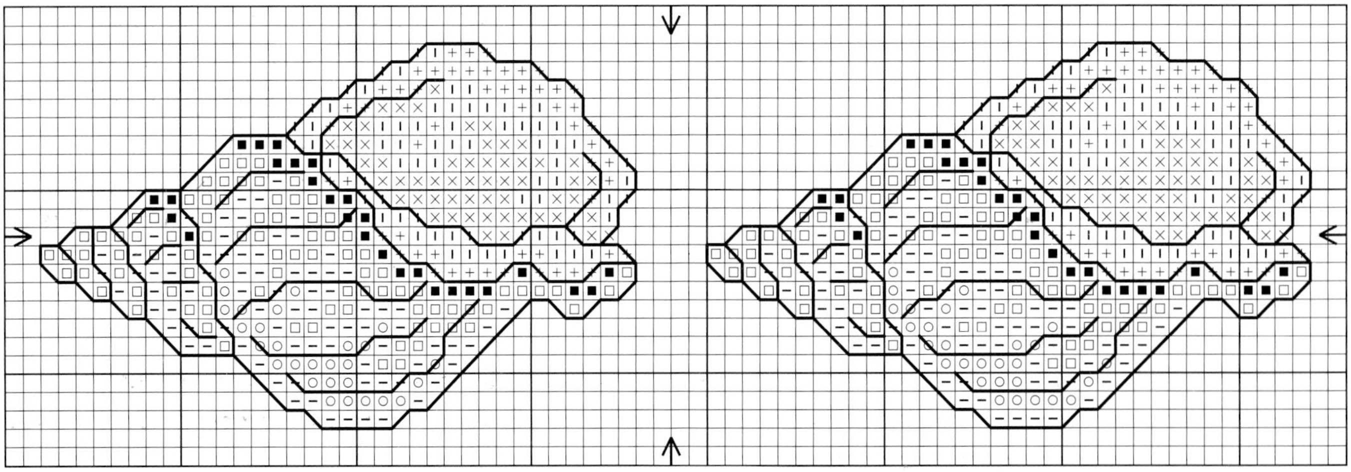

PICTURE

1 Mark the centre of the Aida fabric with tacking.

2 Begin stitching from the centre out using two strands for cross stitch and one for backstitch (chart A). Work each stitch over one fabric block.

3 When completed, remove the tacking and with a cool iron gently press the design from the wrong side.

4 Either frame the design yourself or take to a professional.

GUEST TOWEL

1 Fold the towel in half and stitch a line of tacking across the Aida panel, marking the vertical centre. Using a tape measure, mark the horizontal centre with tacking.

Above: These seashell towels are perfect for a guest bathroom.

2 Using two strands for cross stitch and one for backstitch, begin stitching from the centre out (chart B), then repeat the motif along the band, leaving a gap of four blocks between each shell.

3 When all the stitching has been completed, remove the tacking and with a cool iron gently press the design from the wrong side.

TIP

Do ensure all the loose thread ends are very firmly secured otherwise they may work loose when the towel is washed or used.

Windmill pantry

Inspired by the rustic scenes on Delft pottery these humble little windmills will really brighten up a plain pantry. With a smart shelf edging and trendy patches stitched on to kitchen accessories, the clear blue motifs add a slightly nostalgic quality to your kitchen.

SKILL LEVEL: 1

MEASUREMENTS

Worked on 14-count Aida with each cross stitch worked over one fabric block, the tea towel patch motif measures 4 x 6 cm (1½ x 2½ in). Worked on 18-count Aida with each cross stitch worked over one fabric block, the shelf edging motif (which is repeated to fit the desired length) measures 4.5 x 3 cm (1¾ x 1¼ in).

YOU WILL NEED

For the embroidery
- 20 cm (8 in) white 18-count Aida, divided by the shelf length plus 4 cm (1½ in)
- Two 14 cm (5½ in) squares white 14-count Aida
- Tapestry needle, size 26
- Embroidery hoop
- Scissors
- Contrasting tacking thread
- DMC stranded cottons as listed

To make up the projects
- Basic sewing kit
- Sewing machine (optional)
- White sewing thread
- Acrylic fridge magnet

Colour		Shade	No. of skeins
■	dark blue	796	1
▨	royal blue	798	1
☐	baby blue	809	1

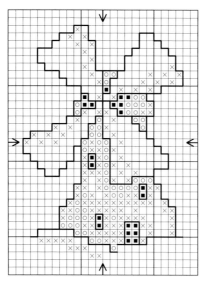

△ Chart A

TEA TOWEL PATCH

1 Fold the 14-count Aida in half horizontally and vertically pressing firmly on the folds to form strong creases.

2 With contrasting cotton, stitch a line of tacking along each crease to mark the fabric centre. Begin stitching from the centre out using two strands for cross stitch and one for backstitch (chart A). Work over one fabric block.

3 When you have completed the stitching, press the design gently on the reverse.

4 Fold over 1 cm (¼ in) all the way round, pin and tack to make a simple square patch.

5 Position the patch on to the tea towel, pin and tack in place. Using either a sewing machine or slipstitching by hand, secure the patch to the tea towel and remove all the tacking thread.

Symbol	Colour	Backstitch	Shade
■	dark blue	◩	796
◎	royal blue		798
⨯	baby blue		809

Above: The patch could also be stitched on to an apron.

▽ Chart B

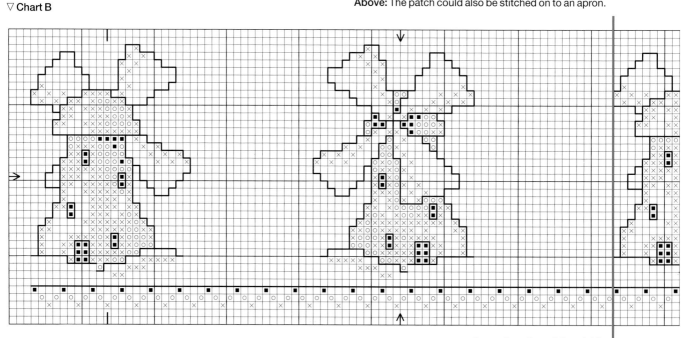

overlap pattern from this point ▷

Left: These shelf edgings add a nostalgic charm to the kitchen.

Below: The fridge magnet is another fun item for the kitchen.

SHELF EDGING

1 Measure the length of your shelf and cut a piece of 18-count Aida 20 cm (8 in) wide by the shelf length, plus 4 cm (1½ in).

2 Mark the centre with tacking.

3 Using one strand of cotton for all stitches and working over one fabric block, begin stitching from the centre out (chart B). Repeat the design along the length of the fabric finishing with a complete motif at least 5 cm (2 in) from either end.

4 When complete, press gently on the reverse. Then, seven blocks from the base of the stitching, fold the bottom third of the fabric behind the embroidery and

tack in place. Either machine or hand stitch above and below the design along the length of the fabric.

5 Turn 2 cm (1 in) under to either side of the design and secure.

6 Turn the top third of the fabric over and press firmly to create a strong fold.

7 Finally using double-sided tape or staples, attach the top part of the fabric to the top of the shelf, letting the windmill border hang down at right angles.

MAGNET

1 Stitch as for the patch and make up the magnet using the supplier's instructions.

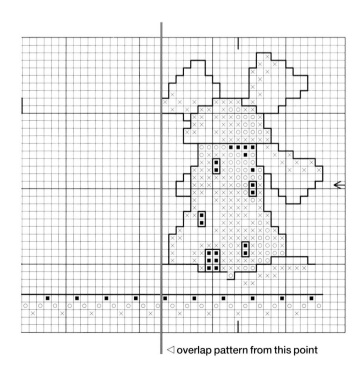

◁ overlap pattern from this point

Green linen teaset

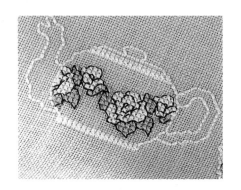

Use these lovely teaset motifs to create something special to accompany your favourite china at teatime. Using backstitch to draw the outlines and cross stitch to create the patterns adds an interesting design twist.

SKILL LEVEL: 2

MEASUREMENTS
Worked on E3609 linen with each cross stitch worked over two fabric threads, the tray cloth motif (which is repeated) measures 15 x 4 cm (6 x 1½ in). The napkin motif measures 6.5 x 4 cm (2½ x 1½ in) and the napkin ring motif measures 9 x 2 cm (3½ x ¾ in).

YOU WILL NEED
For the embroidery
- 50 x 33 cm (20 x 13 in) pale green E3609 Belfast linen
- 15 x 15 cm (6 x 6 in) pale green E3609 Belfast linen
- 32 x 32 cm (13 x 13 in) white E3609 Belfast linen
- Tapestry needle, size 26
- Embroidery hoop
- Scissors
- Contrasting tacking thread
- DMC stranded cottons as listed

To make up the projects
- Sewing machine
- Pins
- Matching sewing thread
- 3 m (10 ft) white bias binding
- Acrylic napkin ring

Colour		Shade	No. of skeins
▨	pale green	164	1
▨	forest green	520	1
☐	white	blanc	1

overlap pattern from this point ▷

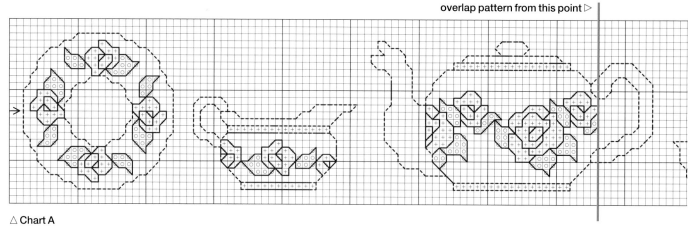

△ Chart A

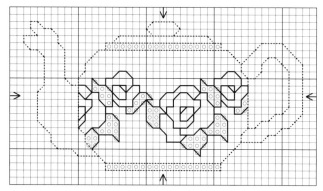

△ Chart B

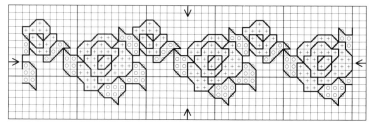

△ Chart C

Symbol	Colour	Backstitch	Shade
○	pale green	⊡	164
	forest green	◨	520
+	white	◪	blanc

Below: White thread on pale green linen creates an unusual effect.

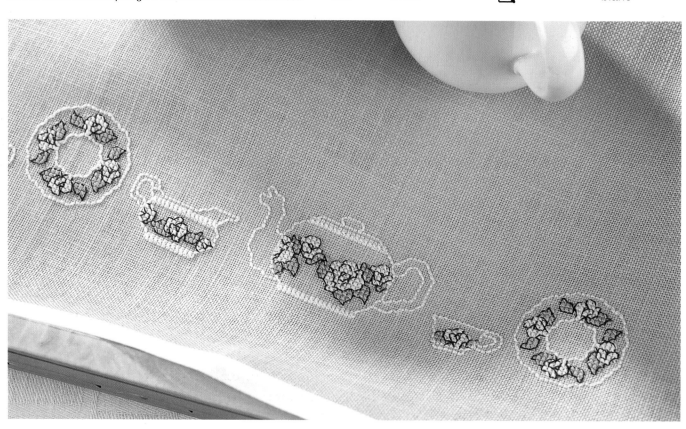

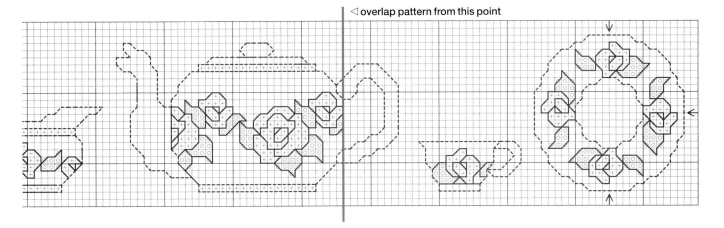

◁ overlap pattern from this point

TRAY CLOTH

1 Cut a 50 x 33 cm (20 x 13 in) piece of pale green linen and bind the edges with white bias binding.

2 Fold the cloth in half across the width and stitch a line of tacking to mark the vertical centre. Next stitch another line of tacking 6 cm (2½ in) from the bottom of the cloth. Where the lines cross marks the central and starting point.

3 Stitch from the centre out using two strands of cotton for cross stitch and the white backstitch, but only one strand for backstitch worked in dark green. Work each stitch over two fabric threads (chart A).

4 Using the centre marks on the chart, stitch the left side of the design first, then repeat to the right.

5 Once you have completed the stitching, remove the central tacking and using a cool iron, press gently.

NAPKIN

1 Cut a 32 cm (13 in) square of white linen and bind the edges as for the tray cloth.

2 Tack two lines approximately 5 cm (2 in) in from the left side and the bottom edge of the napkin. Using where the lines cross as the central mark, work each stitch over two fabric threads (chart B).

3 Use two strands of cotton for cross stitch and pale green backstitch and one strand for the dark green backstitch.

4 Remove the tacking and gently press with a cool iron.

NAPKIN RING

1 Cut a small piece of the pale green linen 8 x 15 cm (3¼ x 6 in) marking the centre with tacking.

2 Stitching from the centre out, use two strands for cross stitch and one strand for backstitch. Work each stitch over two fabric threads (chart C).

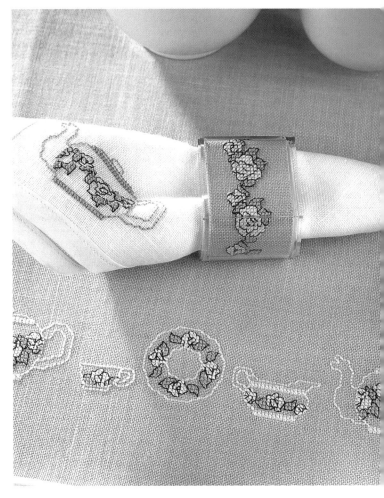

Above: Use this charming teaset for special guests.

3 When complete, back with Vilene and make up the napkin ring using the supplier's instructions.

TIP

The attractive rose border could be repeated along a linen band to adorn any number of teatime accessories, such as a tea towel, tea cosy or even an apron.

Gingham playmat and pram toys

Soft pastel shades of gingham in simple nursery shapes create something different for your new arrival. A soft patchwork play mat and some jingling pram toys will welcome your new born girls and boys.

SKILL LEVEL: 2

MEASUREMENTS

Worked on 11-count Aida with each cross stitch worked over one fabric block, the playmat motifs measure 6 x 6 cm (2½ x 2½ in). Worked on 14-count Aida with each cross stitch worked over one fabric block, the toy motifs measure 5 x 5 cm (2 x 2 in).

YOU WILL NEED

For the embroidery
- Three 18 x 18 cm (7 x 7 in) squares 11-count white Aida
- Three 12 x 12 cm (5 x 5 in) squares 14-count white Aida
- Tapestry needle, size 24
- Tapestry needle, size 26
- Embroidery hoop
- Embroidery scissors
- Contrasting tacking thread
- DMC stranded cottons as listed

To make up the projects
- Basic sewing kit
- Sewing machine
- White sewing thread
- 1 m (40 in) blue gingham
- 50 cm (20 in) yellow gingham
- 75 x 45 cm (30 x 18 in) medium weight wadding
- Fabric pen
- 3 x small bells
- 1.2 m (47 in) cord

Colour		Shade	No. of skeins
☐	lemon	745	1
▨	baby blue	813	1
☐	pale sky	827	1
▨	light green	913	1
☐	palest mint	955	1
☐	baby pink	963	1
☐	candy pink	3326	1
☐	tangerine	3855	1

PATCHWORK PLAY MAT

1 Tack down the centre of the three 11-count Aida squares.

2 With the size 24 needle and working each stitch over one fabric block, use three strands for cross stitch and two for backstitch. Stitch one of each motif in the middle of each square. When completed remove the tacking and gently press with a cool iron.

3 Cut eight 18 cm (7 in) squares from the blue gingham and four from the yellow gingham.

4 With the three stitched squares, arrange them into a chequered pattern, three squares across and five down.

5 Taking a 1.5 cm (⅝ in) seam allowance stitch the squares together in horizontal strips, three at a time.

6 When you have five strips, iron the seams open and stitch the strips together taking care to match the seams.

7 Cut a piece of backing fabric measuring 51 x 81 cm (20 x 32 in) and place it together with the patchwork right sides facing. Put the wadding on the wrong side of the backing fabric and stitch all round tacking a 1.5 cm (⅝ in) seam allowance and leaving a 20 cm (8 in) gap down one side to turn through.

8 Trim the wadding from all edges and corners. Turn right sides out and slipstitch the gap shut. Then carefully machine down the patchwork seams to create a quilted effect.

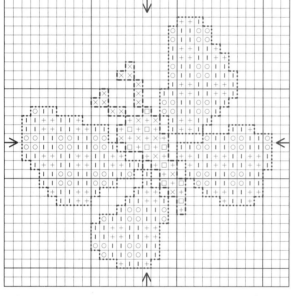

△ Chart A

▷ Chart B

▽ Chart C

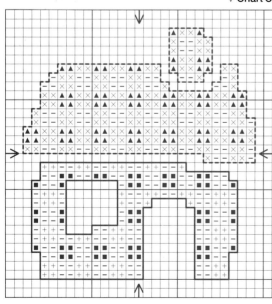

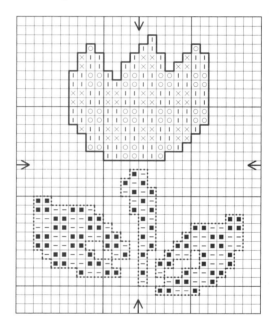

Symbol	Colour	Backstitch	Shade
+	lemon		745
▲	baby blue	◥	813
✕	pale sky		827
■	light green	◢	913
−	palest mint		955
I	baby pink		963
○	candy pink	⋰	3326
□	tangerine	◣	3855

Above: The gingham fabric is echoed in the motif.

PRAM TOYS

1 Tack down the centre of the three 14-count Aida squares.

2 With the size 26 needle and working each stitch over one fabric block, use two strands for cross stitch and one for backstitch.

3 Stitch one of each motif in the middle of each square. When complete remove the tacking and gently press with a cool iron.

4 Cut three circles each measuring 10 cm (4 in) in diameter and three diagonal strips 30 cm (12 in) long and 4 cm (1½ in) wide from the coordinating fabrics.

5 Fold the strips in half lengthways then pin and tack them around the three circles, fold towards the centre.

6 Cut the stitched sample into circles measuring 10 cm (4 in) in diameter. Then with the fabric strips and embroidery on the inside pin, tack and stitch the circles together leaving a 4 cm (1½ in) gap in each one to turn through.

7 Turn the pads right side out and gently press with a cool iron. Fill with wadding and place a single bell within, then slip stitch the gap shut.

8 Take a length of cord and with a needle and thread, stitch the pads on to it at equal intervals.

TIP

If you were stitching this project as a gift you could use one of the motifs on a card to accompany your present.

Above: Stitched on to a length of cord, these pads are lovely toys when tied across a pram.

Architectural drawing

These classical building studies are worked in shades of grey to give them the drawn quality of architectural charcoal sketches. Stitch this motif on to an address book cover to really make a good impression in your entrance hall. An elegantly framed picture adds a classical feel.

SKILL LEVEL: 3

MEASUREMENTS
Worked on Brittney evenweave and with each cross stitch worked over two fabric threads, the picture motif measures 13.5 x 11.5 cm (5½ x 4½ in). The address book motif measures 5 x 6 cm (2 x 2½ in).

YOU WILL NEED
For the embroidery
• 25 x 25 cm (10 x 10 in) white E3270 Brittney evenweave
• 14 x 14 cm (5½ x 5½ in) white E3270 Brittney evenweave
• Tapestry needle, size 26
• Embroidery hoop
• Scissors
• Contrasting tacking thread
• DMC stranded cottons as listed

To make up the projects
• Address book
• 25 cm (10 in) square frame
• Fabric glue or double-sided sticking tape

Colour	Shade	No. of skeins
mid grey	318	2
charcoal	413	1
slate grey	414	1
silver grey	415	2
palest grey	762	2
darkest grey	3799	2
white	blanc	1

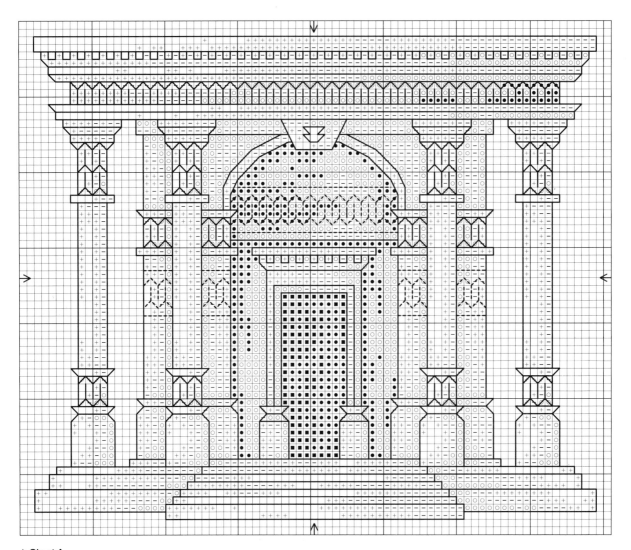

△ Chart A

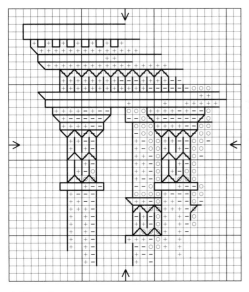

△ Chart B

Symbol	Colour	Backstitch	Shade
○	mid grey		318
■	charcoal		413
●	slate grey		414
−	silver grey		415
+	palest grey		762
	darkest grey	◥	3799
	white	◢	blanc

PICTURE

1 Cut a 25 cm (10 in) square of white evenweave. Mark the centre with tacking.

2 Begin stitching from the centre out working over two fabric threads, using two strands for cross stitch and one for backstitch (chart A).

3 When complete, remove the tacking and press the design gently on the reverse with a cool iron.

4 To finish, frame the design yourself or take to a professional.

ADDRESS BOOK

1 Cut a 14 cm (5½ in) square of white evenweave. Mark the centre with tacking.

2 Begin stitching from the centre out, working over two fabric threads and using two strands for cross stitch and one for backstitch (chart B).

3 When you have completed the stitching, remove the tacking and press the design gently on the reverse with a cool iron.

4 Trim the design to leave 2 cm (1 in) of unworked fabric all the way round the motif and fray the edges by carefully pulling out the end six fabric threads one at a time on all four sides.

5 Leave three threads in place then pull out one more thread to form a border pattern around the edge.

6 Using double-sided tape or fabric glue, secure the design in place on the front of the address book.

TIP

These designs are shown in shades of grey but if you would prefer a softer image why not pick some corresponding shades in sepia tones for an antique print appearance.

Above: Using several shades of grey adds depth and definition to the motif.

Left: The notebook shows just a small section of the main design.

Japanese lady

This elegant Japanese woman glancing shyly over her fan is reminiscent of the prints and drawings of Ancient Japan. With blocks of colour and bold outlines I have tried to recreate this old style, leaving the hands, face and fan unstitched to reflect a print-like quality.

SKILL LEVEL: 3
(quarter and three-quarter stitches used)

MEASUREMENTS
Worked on 28-count Quaker cloth with each cross stitch worked over two fabric threads, the picture motif measures 16 x 8 cm (6 x 3 in). The blossom motif measures 6.5 x 6.5 cm (2½ x 2½ in).

YOU WILL NEED
For the embroidery
- 20 x 30 cm (8 x 12 in) 28-count white Quaker cloth
- 18 x 18 cm (7 x 7 in) 28-count white Quaker cloth
- Tapestry needle, size 26
- Embroidery hoop
- Scissors
- Contrasting tacking thread
- DMC stranded cottons as listed

To make up the projects
- Basic sewing kit
- Silver bowl
- Frame

	Colour	Shade	No. of skeins
■	black	310	1
□	soft aqua	3761	1
□	sand	676	1
■	dark grey	413	1
□	candy pink	962	1
■	cerise	309	1
□	pale pink	963	1
■	grey blue	931	1

PICTURE

1 Fold the piece of 20 x 30 cm (8 x 12 in) evenweave in half horizontally and vertically.

2 With contrasting cotton, stitch a line of tacking along each crease to mark the fabric centre.

3 Begin stitching from the centre out using two strands for cross stitch and one for backstitch. Work each stitch over two fabric threads.

4 When all the stitching has been completed, remove the tacking and with a cool iron, gently press the design from the wrong side.

5 Either frame the design yourself or take to a professional.

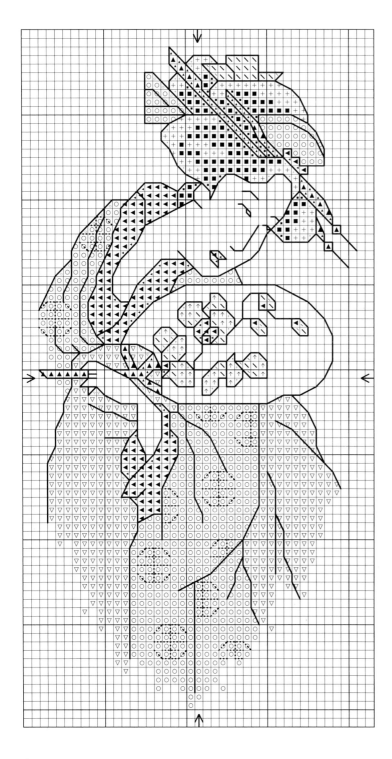

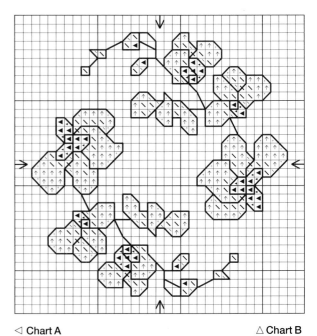

◁ Chart A   △ Chart B

Symbol	Colour	Backstitch	Shade
■	black	◣	310
◯	soft aqua		3761
▲	sand		676
✛	dark grey		413
◥	candy pink		962
◀	cerise		309
↑	pale pink		963
▽	grey blue	◣	931

SILVER BOWL

1 Mark the fabric centre with tacking.

2 Begin stitching from the centre out using two strands for cross stitch and one for backstitch. Work each stitch over two fabric threads.

3 When complete, remove the tacking and press the design from the wrong side.

4 Finally, following the supplier's instructions, fit the finished design in to the bowl lid.

Animal Motifs

Here we show the lighter side of life with some simple
animal, fish and bird designs. You can adorn your kitchen
accessories with quirky farmyard silhouettes, or make eating
at the table fun for children with some comic cat tablemats.

Farmyard animals

Bring a touch of humour to your cooking with these farmyard silhouette kitchen accessories. In dramatic black and white they are the sillier side of chic. Stitched in a row across an Aida band or on a patch, they are simple to create and easy to attach.

SKILL LEVEL: 1

MEASUREMENTS

The tea towel motif (which is repeated to create a border) measures 19 x 4.5 cm (7½ x 1¾ in). Worked on 14-count Aida with each cross stitch worked over one fabric block, the apron patch motif measures 11 x 8 cm (4½ x 3 in). Worked on 11-count Aida with each cross stitch worked over one fabric block, the oven pad motif measures 8 x 7 cm (3 x 2½ in).

YOU WILL NEED

For the embroidery
- 12 x 12 cm (5 x 5 in) 11-count white Aida
- 15 x 12 cm (6 x 5 in) 14-count white Aida
- 5 cm (2 in) Aida band (tea towel width)
- Tapestry needle, size 26
- Embroidery hoop
- Scissors
- Contrasting tacking thread
- Soft pencil
- DMC stranded cottons as listed

To make up the projects
- Basic sewing kit
- Sewing machine
- Matching sewing thread
- Chenille needle, size 26

- Plain tea towel
- Oven pad
- Apron

Colour		Shade	No. of skeins
■	black	310	2

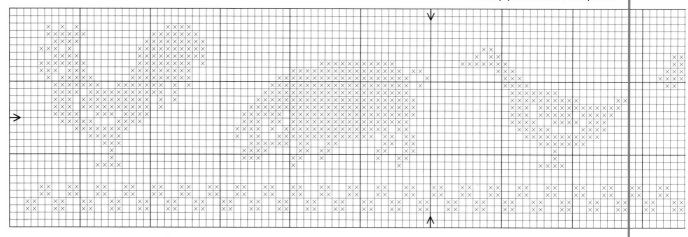

Symbol	Colour	Backstitch	Shade
☒	black	◩	310

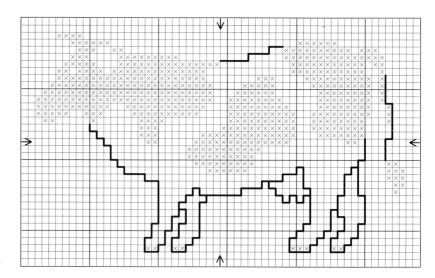

▷ Chart B

TOWEL BAND

1 To calculate the amount of Aida band you will need, measure the width of your tea towel and add 2 cm (1 in).

2 Fold the band in half and, using a contrasting colour, mark the centre with a line of tacking. Fold lengthways to find the horizontal centre and tack another short line. Where the lines cross marks the centre and starting point.

3 Work each stitch over one fabric block using two strands of cotton for cross stitch (chart A).

4 Repeat the design along the band finishing with a complete motif at least 4 cm (1½ in) from either end.

5 Remove the tacking and using a cool iron, press the band gently. Position the Aida band on the tea towel, then pin and tack in place.

6 Finally, either machine or slip stitch in place, remembering to turn under the end of the band to keep it neat.

Below: Black and white silhouettes are simple but stylish.

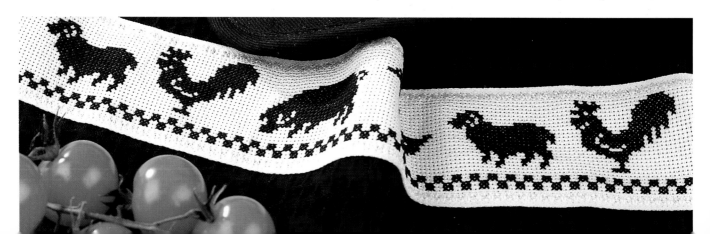

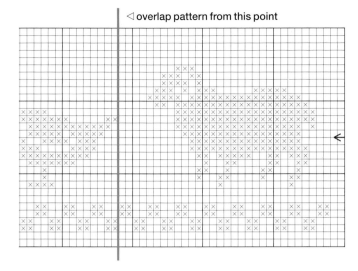

◁ overlap pattern from this point

COW APRON PATCH

1 Cut a piece of 14-count white Aida 15 x 12 cm (6 x 5 in) and mark the centre with tacking.

2 Using two strands of cotton for both cross stitch and backstitch, work over one fabric block (chart B).

3 Fold over 1 cm (½ in) on all sides. Position the patch on the apron then pin and tack in place.

4 Using the chenille needle and two strands of black stranded cotton, backstitch the patch to the apron three fabric blocks from the fold line.

5 Finally remove all tacking and gently press on the reverse using a cool iron.

Above and below: The fun animal patches are easy to stitch and attach.

COCKEREL OVEN PAD

1 Pick one of the small animal silhouettes from chart A and using a soft pencil, mark the centre of your chosen motif on the chart.

2 Cut a 12 cm (5 in) square of 11-count Aida and mark the centre.

3 Using three strands of cotton for the cross stitch, work over one fabric block.

4 Count seven fabric blocks from the design and fold over the excess on all sides.

5 Position the patch on the oven pad, then pin and tack in place. Using the chenille needle and two strands of black stranded cotton, backstitch the patch to the apron three fabric blocks from the fold line.

6 Finally remove all the tacking and gently press on the reverse using a cool iron.

TIP

When stitching patches to pockets do remember to only stitch through one fabric layer or your pocket will be unusable.

Cute cats breakfast set

Breakfast takes on a whole new meaning with this fun table set for children – entice them to the breakfast table with these lovely comic cat accessories. An Aida tablemat, mug and coaster will really brighten up the day.

SKILL LEVEL: 1

MEASUREMENTS

Worked on 11-count Aida with each cross stitch worked over one fabric block, the placemat motif measures 14 x 10 cm (5½ x 4 in) and the coaster motif measures 5 x 4 cm (2 x 1½ in). Worked on 14-count Aida with each cross stitch worked over one fabric block, the mug motif measures 12 x 8 cm (4½ x 3 in).

YOU WILL NEED

For the embroidery
- 40 x 35 cm (16 x 14 in) pale blue 11-count Aida
- 25 x 12 cm (10 x 5 in) pale blue 14-count Aida
- 15 x 15 cm (6 x 6 in) pale blue 11-count Aida
- Tapestry needle, size 26
- Embroidery hoop
- Scissors
- Contrasting tacking thread
- DMC stranded cottons as listed

To make up the projects
- Basic sewing kit
- Sewing machine (optional)
- Matching sewing thread
- Vilene
- Acrylic mug
- Acrylic coaster

Colour		Shade	No. of skeins
■	black	310	1
□	pale pink	605	1
■	orange	722	1
■	ginger	921	1
■	blue	3838	1
□	white	blanc	1

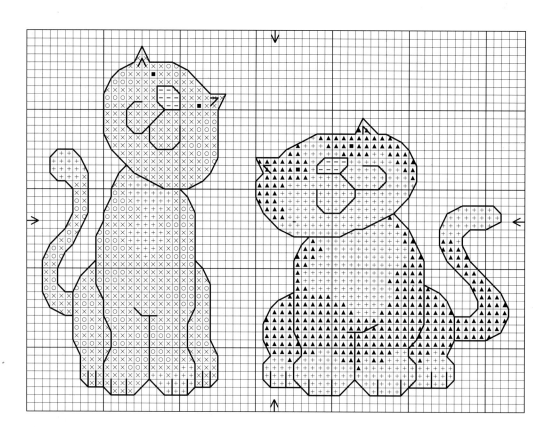

◁ Chart A

Symbol	Colour	Backstitch	Shade
■	black	◻	310
−	pale pink		605
✕	orange		722
○	ginger		921
▲	blue		3838
+	white		blanc

PLACEMAT

1 You will need a piece of 11-count pale blue Aida fabric, approximately 40 x 35 cm (16 x 14 in). Hem the fabric by folding over 1 cm (¼ in) and then another 1.5 cm (½ in). Either machine stitch or hand stitch in place with matching thread.

2 In the bottom left corner stitch two lines of tacking, one horizontally 7 cm (3 in) up from the bottom edge, the other vertically 9 cm (3½ in) in from the left. Use the point where they cross as the design centre.

3 Work each stitch over one fabric block, using three strands of thread for the cross stitch and two for the backstitch (chart A).

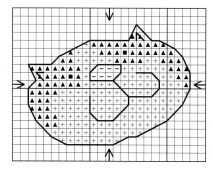

△ Chart B

Left: Acrylic coasters are easy to make up.

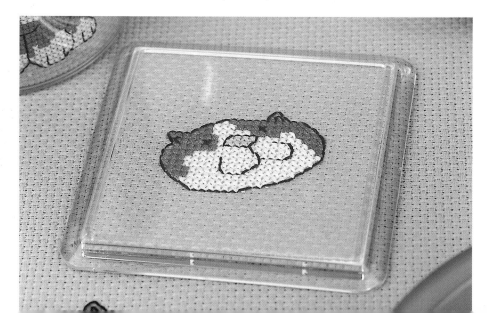

4 When complete remove the tacking and gently press on the reverse with a cool iron.

COASTER

1 For the coaster simply stitch one of the cat's heads (chart B).

2 Cut a small piece of 11-count pale blue Aida, 15 cm (6 in) square and mark the centre with tacking.

3 Stitch the motif using three strands of thread for the cross stitch and two for the backstitch.

4 When complete, remove the tacking and back with Vilene. Then follow the supplier's instructions to make up the coaster.

MUG

1 Mark the centre of a piece of 14-count pale blue Aida measuring 25 x 12 cm (10 x 5 in) with tacking stitches.

2 Working from the centre out, begin stitching using two strands for cross stitch and one for backstitch.

3 When complete, remove the tacking and gently press with a cool iron on the reverse, back with Vilene and make up the mug using supplier's instructions.

Above and below: The placemat and mug will appeal to all children.

Teddy Bear baby set

While awaiting a new arrival, why not fill the time by preparing a few simple gifts? This cosy blanket will be cherished by mother and baby on all those late night feeds, and as the child grows, this bib will not only look nice it will be useful too. A teddy bear rattle with three matching cross stitch hearts is hard to resist.

SKILL LEVEL: 1

MEASUREMENTS
Worked on 11-count Aida with each cross stitch worked over one fabric block, the blanket patch motif measures 10 x 12 cm (4 x 4½ in). The bib motif measures 6 x 7.5 cm (2½ x 3 in) and the rattle motif measures 3 x 1 cm (1 x ¼ in).

YOU WILL NEED
For the embroidery
- Aida bib
- 'Ready to Stitch' Teddy rattle
- 15 x 16 cm (6 x 6½ in) white 11-count Aida
- Tapestry needle, size 26
- Embroidery hoop
- Scissors
- Contrasting tacking thread
- DMC stranded cottons as listed

To make up the projects
- Basic sewing kit
- Sewing machine (optional)
- White sewing thread

Colour		Shade	No. of skeins
	coral	351	1
	pale peach	353	1
	dark brown	433	1
	golden brown	436	1
	light brown	437	1
	light tan	739	1
	baby blue	3839	1
	pale sky	3840	1

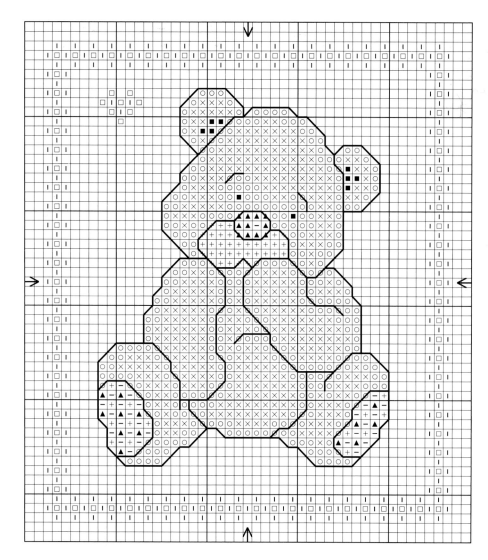

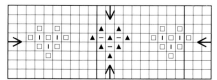

Symbol	Colour	Backstitch	Shade
▲	coral		351
−	pale peach		353
■	dark brown	◩	433
⊙	golden brown		436
✕	light brown		437
+	light tan		739
□	baby blue		3839
I	pale sky		3840

Right: This teddy bear patch is perfect for a cosy blanket.

BLANKET PATCH

1 Mark the centre of the Aida with tacking.

2 Begin stitching from the centre out using three strands for cross stitch and two for backstitch. Work each stitch over one fabric block (chart A).

3 When you have completed the design gently press on the reverse using a cool iron.

4 Count five fabric blocks from the design and fold over the excess Aida on all sides.

5 Position the patch on the blanket, pin and tack in place.

6 Finally, using either machine or hand stitch, secure the Aida patch to the blanket and remove all the tacking.

AIDA BIB

1 Find the bib centre by folding it in half horizontally and vertically. With contrasting cotton, stitch a line of tacking along each crease to mark the centre.

Above: Ready-made Aida items are ideal for making up quick gifts.

2 Omitting the border and little heart, begin stitching from the centre out. Use two strands for the cross stitch and one for the backstitch, working each stitch over one fabric block.

3 Remove the tacking and gently press with a cool iron.

'READY TO STITCH' TEDDY RATTLE

1 Using a tape measure, find the centre of the teddy's bib and mark with tacking.

2 Stitch the three tiny heart shapes (chart B), using two strands for cross stitch. Work each stitch over one fabric block.

3 When the stitching is complete remove the tacking.

Blue bird bed linen

Blue and white is a classic colour combination that works every time – particularly in bedrooms. This crisp white bed linen features swooping blue birds stitched on to pillowcases using waste canvas, as well as on the Aida band on the sheet. A bedside trinket box for precious items is adorned with two birds.

SKILL LEVEL: 1

MEASUREMENTS

Worked on 14-count waste canvas, the pillow motif measures 6 x 4 cm (2½ x 1½ in). The sheet motif (which is repeated to create a border) measures 11 x 5 cm (4½ x 2 in). Worked on Hardanger with each cross stitch worked over one pair of threads, the box motif measures 7.5 x 3 cm (3 x 1¼ in).

YOU WILL NEED
For the embroidery
- Two 10 cm (4 in) squares 14-count waste canvas
- 7.5 cm (3 in) Aida band (sheet width)
- 10 x 15 cm (4 x 6 in) white Hardanger
- Tapestry needle, size 26
- Chenille needle, size 26
- Embroidery hoop
- Scissors
- Contrasting tacking thread
- DMC stranded cottons as listed

To make up the projects
- Basic sewing kit
- Tweezers
- Sewing machine
- White sewing thread

Colour		Shade	No. of skeins
	soft blue	3839	1
	pale sky	3840	2

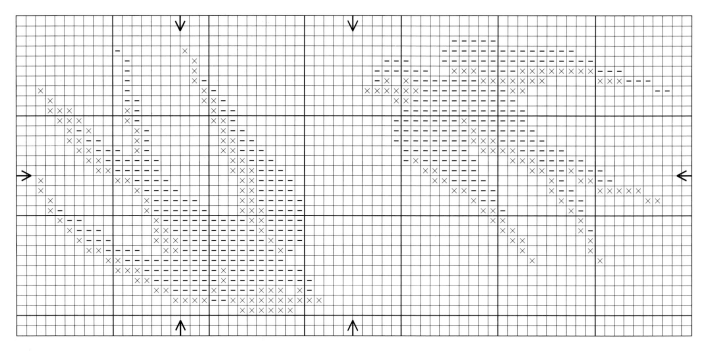

Symbol	Colour	Shade
☒	soft blue	3839
☐	pale sky	3840

SHEET BAND

1 To calculate the amount of Aida band you will need, measure the width of your sheet and add 5 cm (2 in).

2 Fold the band in half and mark the centre with a line of tacking. Fold lengthways to find the horizontal centre and tack another short line, where the lines cross marks the centre and starting point.

3 Using two lengths of stranded cotton in the tapestry needle, cross stitch the first motif from the centre out.

4 Leaving four Aida blocks between each motif, continue left and right along the band until you have approximately 15 cm (6 in) clear at either end. (As long as each gap is the same, you can leave larger spaces between each motif to achieve an airier look.)

5 Once you have completed the stitching, remove the tacking and use a cool iron press the band. Pin and tack the band about 5 cm (2 in) from the top of the sheet, with the design upside down so that when the sheet is turned over it will read the correct way.

6 Finally machine or slip stitch in place, remembering to turn in the end of the band to keep it neat.

Left: The motifs are spaced evenly along the Aida band.

PILLOW CASES

1 Cut a 10 cm (4 in) square of waste canvas and mark the centre.

2 Position the canvas where you want your bird motif to be and tack into place, remembering to stitch through only one side of the case.

3 Use a small embroidery hoop to keep the canvas and pillow case layer taut. Stitch using two strands of cotton and the chenille needle.

4 When the motif is complete, remove the tacking and damp down the waste canvas. Pull the canvas threads out one at a time using tweezers and then gently press with a cool iron.

VARIATION

To add interest to your bedding you could stitch the motifs in white on a coordinating blue pillowcase.

JEWELLERY BOX

1 Mark the centre of the Hardanger with tacking and using the centre arrows on the chart work from the centre out.

2 Use one length of stranded cotton over one pair of Hardanger threads.

3 When you have completed the stitching remove the tacking and gently press.

4 Make up the box pad using the supplier's instructions.

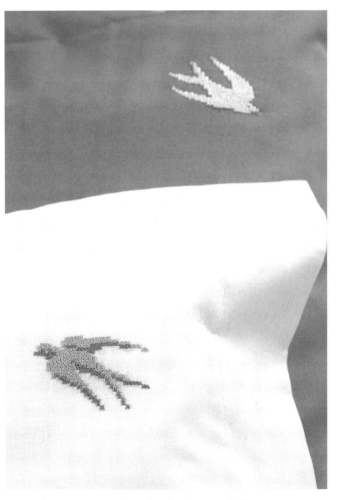

Above: Choose a contrasting colour for the second pillowcase.

Right: This little box is perfect for special trinkets and secret items.

Seaside bathroom

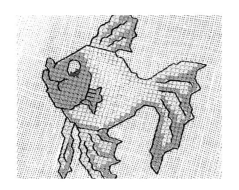

Jazz up your bathtime with these colourful accessories featuring a happy purple seahorse and jolly turquoise fish. Simple patches on colour-coordinating towels look really fresh and modern. You could also invest in some acrylic accessories and give your whole bathroom an ocean theme.

SKILL LEVEL: 2

MEASUREMENTS

Worked on 32-count linen with each cross stitch worked over two fabric threads, the motifs measure 8 x 7 cm (3 x 2 ¾ in) and 9 x 4.5 cm (3½ x 2 in).

YOU WILL NEED

For the embroidery
- Four 15 cm (6 in) squares baby blue 32-count E3609 Belfast linen
- Tapestry needle, size 26
- Embroidery hoop
- Scissors
- Contrasting tacking thread
- DMC stranded cottons as listed

To make up the projects
- Basic sewing kit
- Sewing machine (optional)
- Matching sewing thread
- Acrylic pot
- Acrylic frame

Colour		Shade	No. of skeins
■	dark blue	311	1
□	lilac	341	1
▨	turquoise	807	1
■	navy	823	1
▨	purple	3746	1
▨	pale aqua	3761	1

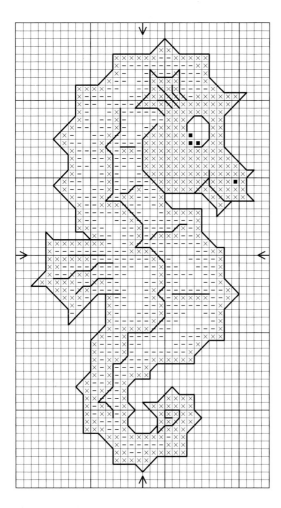

▷ Chart A

TOWEL PATCHES

1 Fold the linen square in half horizontally and vertically pressing firmly on the folds to form strong creases. Stitch a line of tacking along each crease to mark the fabric centre.

2 Begin stitching from the centre out using two strands for cross stitch and one for backstitch. Work over two fabric threads (chart A).

3 When you have completed the stitching, remove the tacking and press.

4 Measure 1.5 cm (½ in) away from the design and fold over the excess fabric on all sides, pinning and tacking in place. This will make up a simple patch.

5 Position the patch on the towel and pin, then tack.

6 Finally, using either a sewing machine or slipstitching by hand, secure the linen to the towel. Remove all the tacking thread.

Above: Choose a towel that matches the colours of the motif.

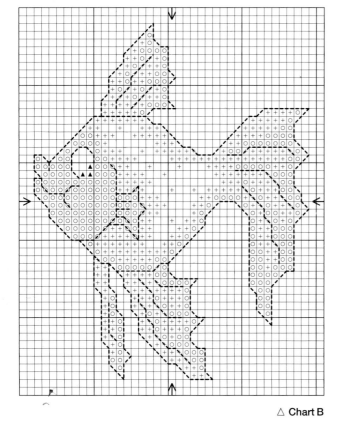

△ Chart B

Symbol	Colour	Backstitch	Shade
▲	dark blue	◹	311
⊟	lilac		341
⊙	turquoise		807
■	navy	◺	823
☒	purple		3746
⊞	pale aqua		3761

Left: A toothmug and picture frame add to the set.

Below: A seahorse greetings card.

ACRYLIC ACCESSORIES

1 Mark the centre of the linen squares with tacking.

2 Begin stitching from the centre out using two strands for cross stitch and one for backstitch. Work over two fabric threads (chart B).

3 When the stitching is complete, remove the tacking and press the design from the reverse.

4 To finish back the linen with Vilene to prevent fraying, trim and make up using the supplier's instructions.

TIP

If your bathroom has a specific colour scheme it is easy to change the colour of these motifs. Just pick three shades of the same colour making sure the darkest one will give a strong enough outline to pick out the detail.

VARIATION

These fun motifs are perfect if you fancy making your own cards. Simply stitch the motif as above, trim to 1 cm (¼ in) all round, fray the edges and stick on to a blank card.

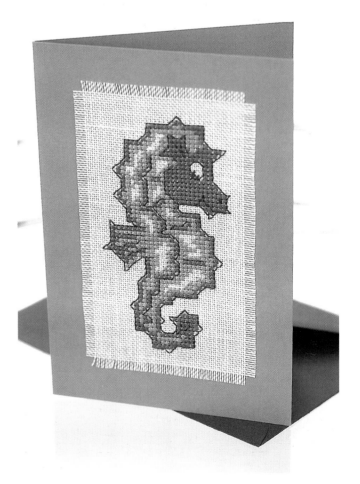

Geometric Motifs

Simple geometric designs are often the most effective, especially when worked in strong, contrasting colours. Repeated patterns, whether a grouping of hearts or a Turkish design, are pleasing to the eye and will lift a whole range of items, from table linen to towels.

Blue and white sampler

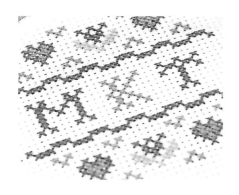

This lovely wall hanging adds a modern touch to the traditional sampler. Stitched in clear blue shades, it has a fresh Scandinavian feel and with matching notebook and personalised wooden bowl, would make a lovely gift for a special friend. Simply add your loved one's initials.

SKILL LEVEL: 1

MEASUREMENTS

Worked on Aida band, the wall hanging design measures 16 x 9 cm (6 x 3½ in). Worked on 14-count Aida with each cross stitch worked over one fabric block, the wooden pot motif measures 7 x 7 cm (2¾ x 2¾ in). Worked on 16-count linen with each cross stitch worked over one fabric thread, the notebook motif measures 6 x 11 cm (2½ x 4½ in).

YOU WILL NEED

For the embroidery
- 30 cm (12 in) 14 cm (5½ in) wide Aida band
- 14 cm (5½ in) 14-count white Aida
- 15 x 10 cm (6 x 4 in) 16-count white linen
- Tapestry needle, size 26
- Embroidery hoop
- Scissors
- Contrasting tacking thread
- DMC stranded cottons as listed

To make up the projects
- Basic sewing kit
- Sewing machine (optional)
- White sewing thread
- Bell pull rods
- Wooden pot
- Small notebook
- Glue or double-sided sticking tape

Colour		Shade	No. of skeins
■	royal blue	798	1
■	light blue	799	1
□	pale sky	800	1

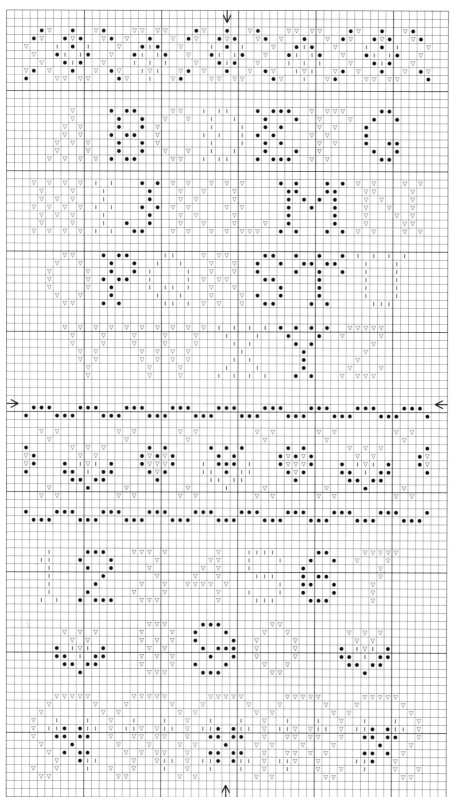

Symbol	Colour	Shade
●	royal blue	798
▽	light blue	799
I	pale sky	800

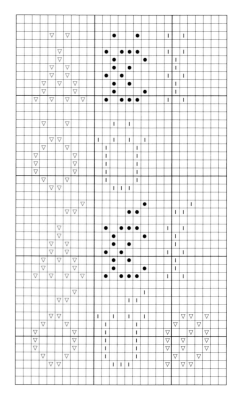

△ **Chart B:** Additional letters and accents are easy to create. Here are some of the most common ones.

△ **Chart A**

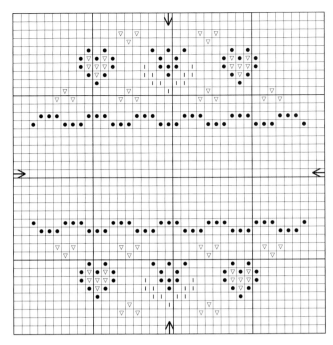

△ Chart C

Above: Add the initials of a loved one for a special gift.

WALL HANGING

1 Fold the Aida band in half vertically and horizontally then mark the creases with tacking. Using two strands of cotton in the needle and working over one fabric block, begin stitching from the centre out (chart A).

2 When the sampler is complete, remove the tacking and with a cool iron gently press the design on the reverse.

3 Fold over 1 cm (½ in), then another 3 cm (1½ in) at both ends. Pin and tack and either machine or hand stitch in place using white sewing thread. This forms the channels through which to slot the bell pull rods.

4 Finally slip the bell pull rods into place and hang.

PERSONALIZED WOODEN BOWL

1 Personalizing the design is easy. Referring to the alphabet on the sampler chart and using a soft pencil, simply draw your chosen initials on to the chart.

2 Fold the Aida in half vertically and horizontally then mark the creases with tacking.

3 Using two strands of cotton in the needle and working over one fabric block, begin stitching from the centre out (chart C).

4 When you have completed the stitching, remove the tacking and gently press the design on the reverse.

5 Make up the pot using the supplier's instructions.

Right: Keep all your secrets in this notebook.

NOTEBOOK

1 Mark the centre of the linen with tacking.

2 Use one strand of cotton in the needle and work over one fabric thread. Be careful not to pull your stitches too tight, as they will slip between the weave.

3 Remove the tacking and with a cool iron, gently press on the reverse.

4 Trim to 1 cm (½ in) outside the design, pull out a couple of fabric threads to form a fringed edge and stick the embroidery to the book using glue or sticky tape.

Playing card motifs

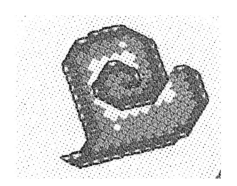

Add a touch of fun to your boudoir with these girly playing card motifs. Stitch the heart, club, diamond and spade in turn along a band to adorn the top of a sheet or in a square to patch on to a fluffy cushion. And why not use a single motif to personalize your own notebook?

SKILL LEVEL: 1

MEASUREMENTS
Worked on Aida band with each cross stitch worked over one fabric block, the sheet motif (which is repeated) measures 21 x 4 cm (8 x 1¾ in). Worked on 22-count Hardanger with each cross stitch worked over two pairs of threads, the cushion patch motif measures 11 x 11 cm (4½ x 4½ in) and the notebook motif measures 4.5 x 5 cm (1¾ x 2 in).

YOU WILL NEED

For the embroidery
- 16 x 16 cm (6 x 6 in) 22-count white Hardanger
- 12 x 12 cm (5 x 5 in) 22-count white Hardanger
- 5 cm (2 in) Aida band (sheet width)
- Tapestry needle, size 26
- Tapestry needle, size 24
- Embroidery hoop
- Scissors
- Contrasting tacking thread
- Soft pencil
- DMC stranded cottons as listed

To make up the projects
- Basic sewing kit
- Sewing machine
- Matching sewing thread
- Bias binding
- Plain sheet
- Fleece cushion cover

Colour		Shade	No. of skeins
■	lavender	155	2
□	lilac	210	2
▨	coral	335	2
▢	pink	3608	2

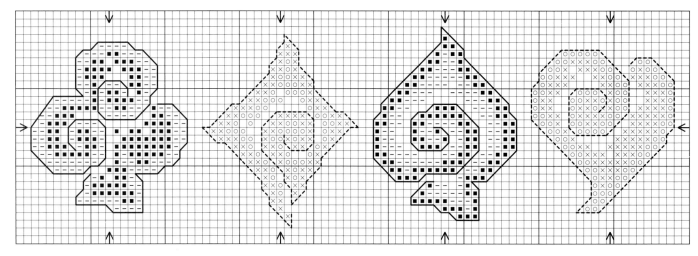

△ Chart A

▽ Chart B

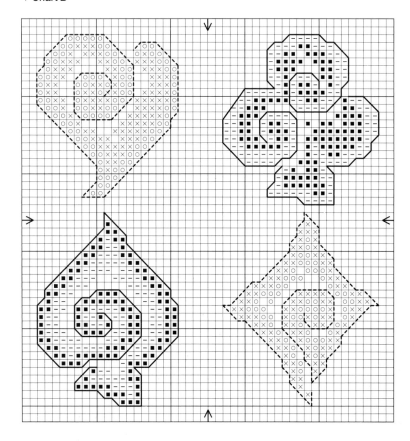

Symbol	Colour	Backstitch	Shade
■	lavender	↘	155
−	lilac		210
○	coral	◥	335
⊠	pink		3608

Above: A pretty cushion patch.

CUSHION PATCH

1 Cut a 16 cm (6½ in) square of white Hardanger and mark the centre with tacking.

2 With the size 24 tapestry needle and using four strands of cotton in the needle for the cross stitch and two for the backstitch, stitch the design from the centre out (chart B). Work each stitch over two pairs of fabric threads.

3 With the motifs complete, remove the tacking and gently press on the reverse using a cool iron.

4 Position the stitched square centrally on the cushion cover. Counting six pairs of fabric threads in from the edge, pin, tack and machine stitch in place.

5 Finally pull four pairs of fabric threads away on all sides to create a fringed effect around the edge of the patch.

NOTEBOOK

1 Stitch as for cushion patch using only one motif on a 7.5 cm (3 in) square of white Hardanger.

2 Attach to the book, as desired.

Above: Some notebooks have a cut-out panel.

Above: The motifs are evenly spaced along the Aida band.

SHEET BAND

1 To calculate the amount of Aida band you will need measure the width of your sheet and add 5 cm (2 in).

2 Fold the band in half and mark the centre with a line of tacking. Stitch further lines at 6 cm (2¼ in) intervals to either side continuing along the band.

3 Fold lengthways to find the horizontal centre and tack a series of short lines crossing the first ones. Where the lines cross marks the centre and starting point for each motif.

4 Using two lengths of stranded cotton for cross stitch and one for backstitch, work each stitch over one fabric block. Stitch the motifs in turn across the band (*spaces between motifs not shown on chart*)

5 Remove the tacking and, using a cool iron, press the band gently on the reverse.

6 Pin and tack the band about 9 cm (3½ in) from the top of the sheet, with the design upside down so that when the sheet is turned over it will read correctly. Finally machine or slip stitch in place, remembering to turn in the ends to keep it neat.

Red and white table linen

Use a simple sampler motif to create some stylish table linens. A red design on crisp white fabric gives this dramatic table runner with matching accessories a touch of modern flare and brightens up your dining table. With hundreds of thread colours to choose from, you could match any colour scheme.

SKILL LEVEL: 2

MEASUREMENTS
Worked on 28-count Brittney evenweave with each cross stitch worked over two fabric threads, the table runner motif measures 32 x 8 cm (12½ x 3 in). The napkin motif measures 5 x 5 cm (2 x 2 in) and the napkin ring motif measures 2.5 x 2 cm (1 x ¾ in).

NOTE
Quantities given are enough for 1 runner, 4 napkins and 4 napkin rings.

YOU WILL NEED
For the embroidery
• 105 cm (41½ in) E3270, 28-count white Brittney evenweave
• Tapestry needle, size 26
• Embroidery hoop
• Scissors
• Contrasting tacking thread
• DMC stranded cottons as listed

To make up the projects
• Sewing machine
• Pins
• White sewing thread
• Tape measure
• Acrylic napkin rings

Colour		Shade	No. of skeins
■	red	321	3

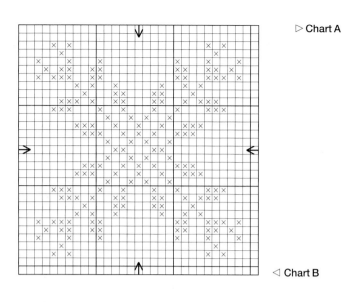

▷ Chart A

◁ Chart B

Symbol	Colourh	Shade
☒	red	321

TABLE RUNNER

1 Cut a length of fabric 140 x 45 cm (55 x 18 in) and hem by folding over 1 cm (½ in) then another 1.5 cm (1 in). Machine stitch in place.

2 Fold the completed table runner in half lengthways and mark the central line with tacking.

3 Stitch two lines of tacking 8 cm (3 in) in from either end and two more at equally spaced distances, about 35 cm (14 in) apart, so that when complete you will have four evenly spaced lines along the table runner. This will mark the centre of each row of motifs.

4 Using two strands of cotton in the needle and starting from the centre out stitch four rows of three motifs across the runner (chart A).

5 When you have completed all the stitching, remove the tacking and gently press with a cool iron on the reverse of the cloth.

Below: The chic table runner has a geometric design of hearts.

◁ overlap pattern from this point

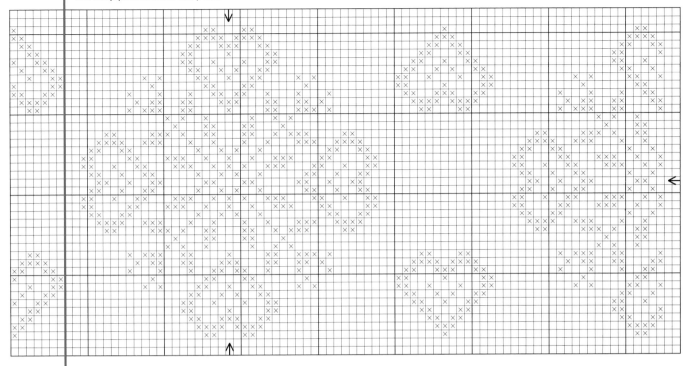

NAPKIN

1 Hem a 30 cm (12 in) square of fabric in the same way as for the table runner.

2 In one corner, tack two short lines approximately 6 cm (2¼ in) in from the edges. Use where they cross as the centre mark.

3 Using two strands of cotton stitch the motif (chart B).

4 Remove the tacking and gently press on the reverse side with a cool iron.

NAPKIN RING

1 Cut a small piece of fabric 8 x 15 cm (3¼ x 6 in).

2 Stitch a single heart shape from chart A in the centre, using two strands of cotton.

3 When you have completed the stitching, back with Vilene and make up the napkin ring using the supplier's instructions.

TIP

If red is not the right colour for your dining room, simply pick up a stranded cotton shade card and choose the one that will set off your table best. There are hundreds of shades to choose from – you might even want to try a variegated or metallic thread.

Right: A napkin and napkin ring complete the set.

Turkish bathroom

Spice up your bathroom with these enchanting floral motifs. Inspired by patterns found on Turkish textiles and ceramics, they will add a touch of eastern promise to your bathing. Cool blues are perfect for a bathroom and when stitched on to crisp, white linen, look fresh and modern.

SKILL LEVEL: 2

MEASUREMENTS

Worked on 32-count linen with each cross stitch worked over two fabric threads, the soap bag motif measures 8.5 x 10 cm (3½ x 4 in). The towel motif (which is repeated along the width of the towel) measures 14.5 x 3 cm (5½ x 1½ in).

YOU WILL NEED

For the embroidery
- 43 x 43 cm (17 x 17 in) 32-count white Belfast linen
- Guest towel with Aida panel
- Tapesty needle, size 26
- Embroidery hoop
- Scissors
- Contrasting tacking thread
- DMC stranded cottons as listed

To make up the projects
- Basic sewing kit
- Sewing machine
- White sewing thread
- 1 m (3 ft) cord

Colour		Shade	No. of skeins
■	dark blue	796	1
■	royal blue	798	1
■	baby blue	809	1
□	palest aqua	747	1
■	aqua	964	1

Symbol	Colour	Shade
■	dark blue	796
✕	royal blue	798
−	baby blue	809
○	palest aqua	747
▲	aqua	964

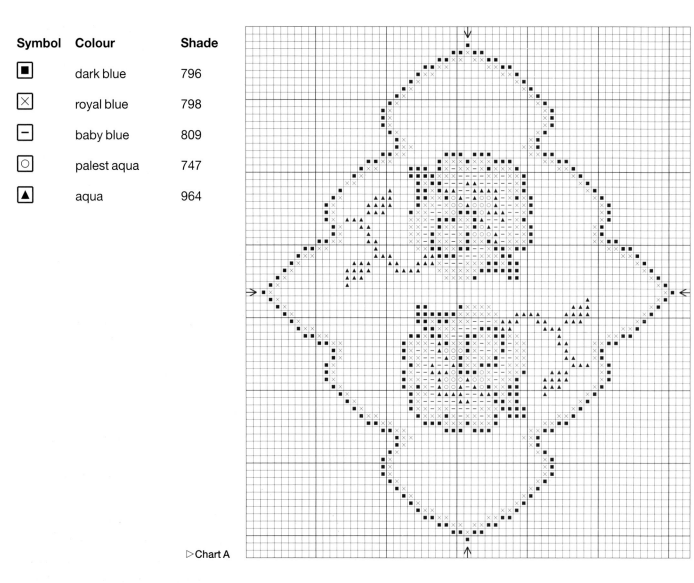

▷Chart A

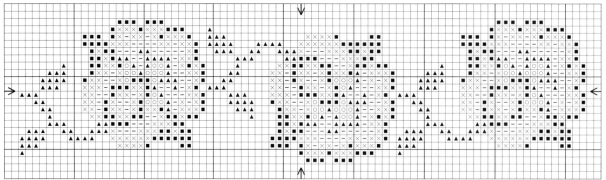

△ Chart B

SOAP BAG

1 Fold the linen in half and mark the crease with a line of tacking. With the fabric laid out so the line sits vertically, measure 12 cm (4½ in) up from the bottom and stitch another line of tacking horizontally across the first. Where the lines cross marks the design centre.

2 Using two strands of cotton, begin stitching from the centre out (chart A).

3 When you have completed the stitching, remove the tacking and gently press on the reverse with a cool iron.

4 With the fabric face down, fold 10 cm (4 in) over from the top. Then, using white thread, machine stitch two parallel lines across the linen, 3 cm (1 in) apart and 6 cm (2¼ in) from the top. This will form the channel through which to thread the cord.

5 Fold the fabric horizontally, design facing inward, and, taking a 1.5 cm (½ in) seam allowance, machine stitch down the edge, remembering to leave a gap between the parallel rows of stitching. Press open the seam and zig-zag or oversew the edges to prevent fraying.

6 With this seam directly opposite the stitching and the design positioned centrally on the front, take a 1.5 cm (½ in) seam allowance and machine stitch the bottom of the bag. Zig-zag or oversew the edges to prevent fraying.

7 Turn the bag right side out and press. Then thread the cord through the channel.

Right: This blue design is inspired by Turkish tiles and ceramics.

Above: This drawstring bag is perfect for soap or cotton wool.

GUEST TOWEL

1 Fold the towel in half and stitch a line of tacking across the Aida panel, marking the vertical centre. Using a tape measure, find the horizontal centre and mark with tacking.

2 Using two strands of cotton, begin stitching from the centre out (chart B), repeating the design along the band and finishing at either end with a complete motif.

3 Remove the tacking and with a cool iron, gently press on the reverse.

TIP

Do ensure all the thread ends are very firmly secured otherwise they may work loose when the towel is washed or used.

DMC chart

Shade no.	Column no.	Shade no.	Column no.	Shade no.	Column no.	Shade no.	Column no.	Shade no.	Column no.	Shade no.	Column no.	Shade no.	Column no.
B5200	17	334	6	598	7	783	12	922	14	3072	17	3805	4
Blanc	17	335	2	600	4	791	5	924	8	3078	13	3806	4
Ecru	17	336	6	601	4	792	5	926	8	3325	6	3807	5
48	19	340	5	602	4	793	5	927	8	3326	2	3808	7
51	20	341	5	603	4	794	5	928	8	3328	1	3809	7
52	19	347	1	604	4	796	5	930	6	3340	13	3810	7
53	20	349	1	605	4	797	5	931	6	3341	13	3811	7
57	19	350	1	606	13	798	5	932	6	3345	9	3812	7
61	20	351	1	608	13	799	5	934	10	3346	9	3813	8
62	19	352	1	610	12	800	5	935	10	3347	9	3814	8
67	19	353	1	611	12	801	16	936	10	3348	9	3815	8
69	20	355	15	612	12	806	7	937	10	3350	2	3816	8
75	19	356	15	613	12	807	7	938	16	3354	2	3817	8
90	20	367	9	632	15	809	5	939	6	3362	11	3818	9
91	19	368	9	640	17	813	5	943	8	3363	11	3819	11
92	20	369	9	642	17	814	1	945	14	3364	11	3820	12
93	19	370	11	644	17	815	1	946	13	3371	16	3821	12
94	20	371	11	645	17	816	1	947	13	3607	4	3822	12
95	19	372	11	646	17	817	1	948	15	3608	4	3823	13
99	19	400	14	647	17	818	2	950	15	3609	4	3824	13
101	20	402	14	648	17	819	2	951	14	3685	3	3825	14
102	19	407	15	666	1	820	5	954	9	3687	3	3826	14
103	19	413	18	676	12	822	17	955	9	3688	3	3827	14
104	20	414	18	677	12	823	6	956	2	3689	3	3828	12
105	20	415	18	680	12	824	5	957	2	3705	1	3829	12
106	20	420	12	699	10	825	5	958	7	3706	1	3830	15
107	19	422	12	700	10	826	5	959	7	3708	1	3831	2
108	20	433	16	701	10	827	5	961	2	3712	1	3832	2
111	20	434	16	702	10	828	5	962	2	3713	1	3833	2
112	19	435	16	703	10	829	11	963	2	3716	2	3834	3
113	19	436	16	704	10	830	11	964	7	3721	3	3835	3
114	20	437	16	712	16	831	11	966	9	3722	3	3836	3
115	19	444	13	718	4	832	11	970	13	3726	3	3837	4
116	19	445	13	720	14	833	11	971	13	3727	3	3838	5
121	19	451	15	721	14	834	11	972	13	3731	2	3839	5
122	20	452	15	722	14	838	16	973	13	3733	2	3840	5
123	20	453	15	725	13	839	16	975	14	3740	3	3841	7
124	19	469	10	726	13	840	16	976	14	3743	3	3842	7
125	20	470	10	727	13	841	16	977	14	3746	5	3843	6
126	19	471	10	729	12	842	16	986	9	3747	5	3844	6
208	4	472	10	730	11	844	17	987	9	3750	6	3845	6
209	4	498	1	731	11	869	12	988	9	3752	6	3846	6
210	4	500	8	732	11	890	9	989	9	3753	6	3847	7
211	4	501	8	733	11	891	2	991	8	3755	6	3848	7
221	3	502	8	734	11	892	2	992	8	3756	6	3849	7
223	3	503	8	738	16	893	2	993	8	3760	7	3850	8
224	3	504	8	739	16	894	2	995	6	3761	7	3851	8
225	3	517	7	740	13	895	9	996	6	3765	7	3852	12
300	14	518	7	741	13	898	16	3011	11	3766	7	3853	14
301	14	519	7	742	13	899	2	3012	11	3768	8	3854	14
304	1	520	10	743	13	900	13	3013	11	3770	14	3855	14
307	13	522	10	744	13	902	3	3021	17	3772	15	3856	14
309	2	523	10	745	13	904	10	3022	17	3773	15	3857	15
310	18	524	10	746	12	905	10	3023	17	3774	15	3858	15
311	6	535	17	747	7	906	10	3024	17	3776	14	3859	15
312	6	543	16	754	15	907	10	3031	16	3777	15	3860	15
315	3	550	4	758	15	909	9	3032	17	3778	15	3861	15
316	3	552	4	760	1	910	9	3033	17	3779	15	3862	16
317	18	553	4	761	1	911	9	3041	3	3781	16	3863	16
318	18	554	4	762	18	912	9	3042	3	3782	17	3864	16
319	9	561	8	772	9	913	9	3045	12	3787	17	3865	17
320	9	562	8	775	6	915	4	3046	12	3790	16	3866	17
321	1	563	8	776	2	917	4	3047	12	3799	18		
322	6	564	8	778	3	918	14	3051	10	3801	1		
326	2	580	11	780	12	919	14	3052	10	3802	3		
327	4	581	11	781	12	920	14	3053	10	3803	3		
333	5	597	7	782	12	921	14	3064	15	3804	4		

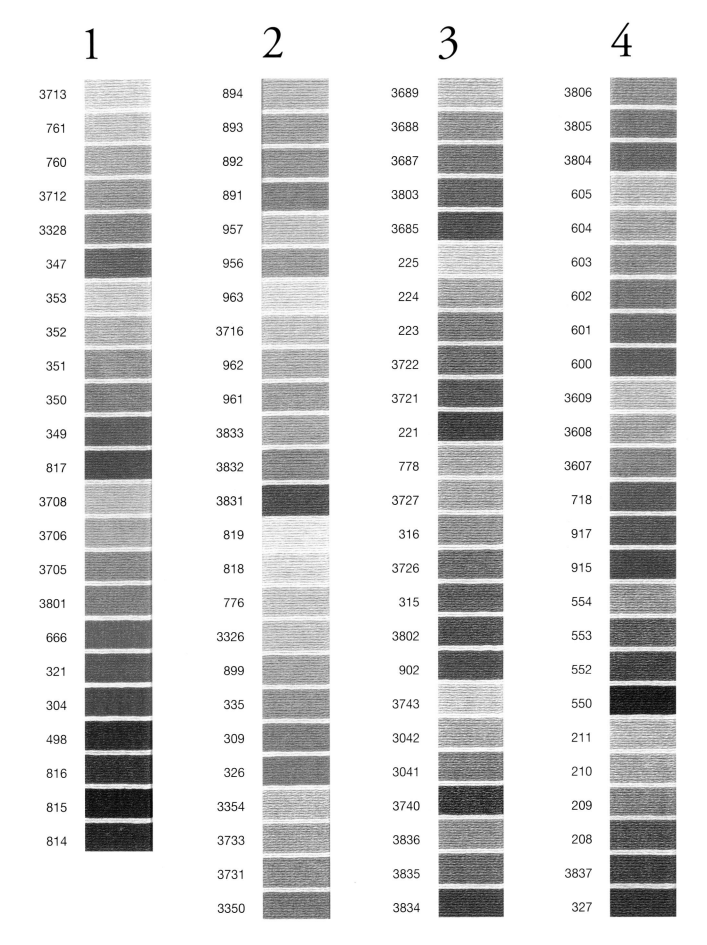

1

3713
761
760
3712
3328
347
353
352
351
350
349
817
3708
3706
3705
3801
666
321
304
498
816
815
814

2

894
893
892
891
957
956
963
3716
962
961
3833
3832
3831
819
818
776
3326
899
335
309
326
3354
3733
3731
3350

3

3689
3688
3687
3803
3685
225
224
223
3722
3721
221
778
3727
316
3726
315
3802
902
3743
3042
3041
3740
3836
3835
3834

4

3806
3805
3804
605
604
603
602
601
600
3609
3608
3607
718
917
915
554
553
552
550
211
210
209
208
3837
327

Exclusive numbering system of DMC © 2002

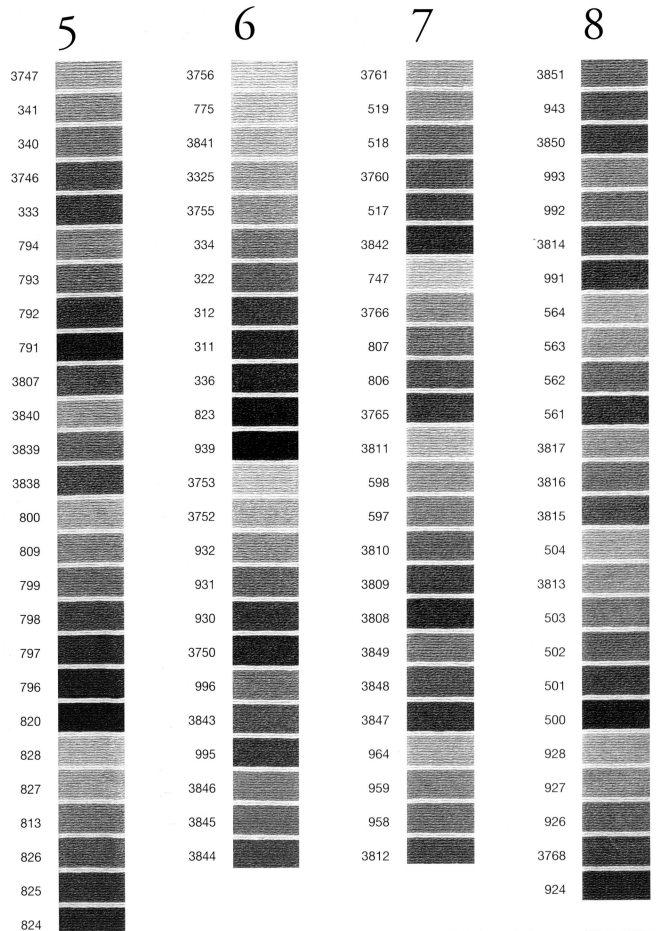

5

3747
341
340
3746
333
794
793
792
791
3807
3840
3839
3838
800
809
799
798
797
796
820
828
827
813
826
825
824

6

3756
775
3841
3325
3755
334
322
312
311
336
823
939
3753
3752
932
931
930
3750
996
3843
995
3846
3845
3844

7

3761
519
518
3760
517
3842
747
3766
807
806
3765
3811
598
597
3810
3809
3808
3849
3848
3847
964
959
958
3812

8

3851
943
3850
993
992
3814
991
564
563
562
561
3817
3816
3815
504
3813
503
502
501
500
928
927
926
3768
924

Exclusive numbering system of DMC © 2002

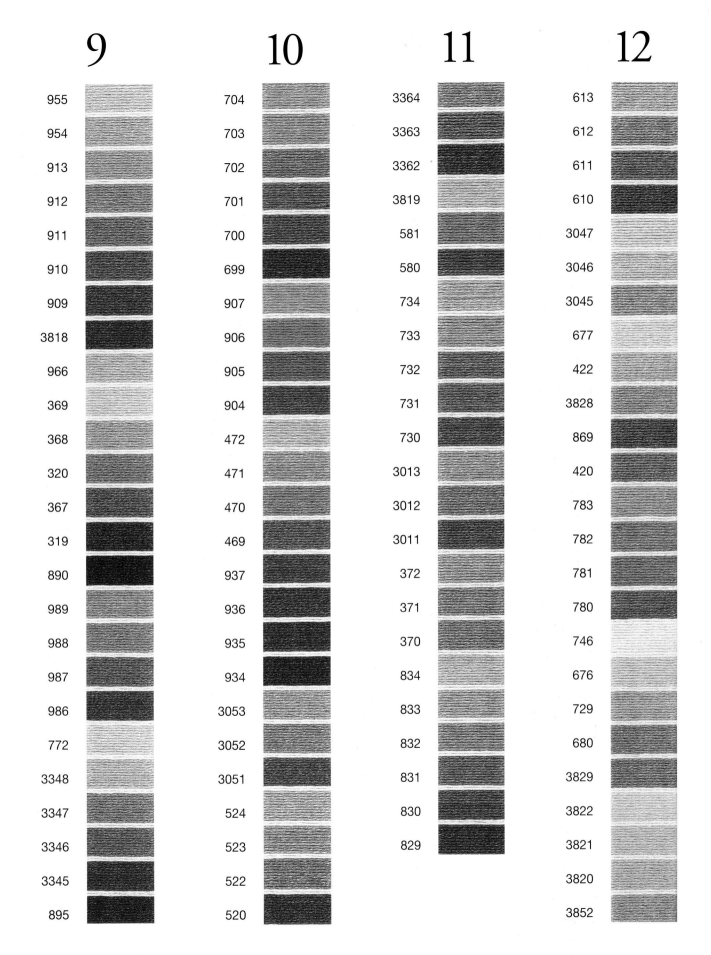

9

955
954
913
912
911
910
909
3818
966
369
368
320
367
319
890
989
988
987
986
772
3348
3347
3346
3345
895

10

704
703
702
701
700
699
907
906
905
904
472
471
470
469
937
936
935
934
3053
3052
3051
524
523
522
520

11

3364
3363
3362
3819
581
580
734
733
732
731
730
3013
3012
3011
372
371
370
834
833
832
831
830
829

12

613
612
611
610
3047
3046
3045
677
422
3828
869
420
783
782
781
780
746
676
729
680
3829
3822
3821
3820
3852

Exclusive numbering system of DMC © 2002

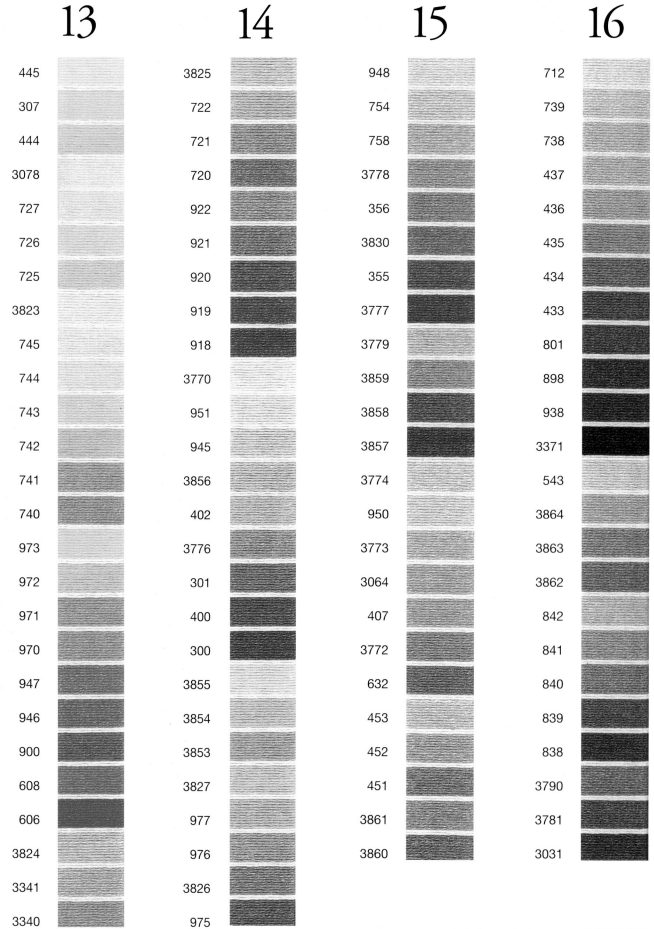

13

| 445 |
| 307 |
| 444 |
| 3078 |
| 727 |
| 726 |
| 725 |
| 3823 |
| 745 |
| 744 |
| 743 |
| 742 |
| 741 |
| 740 |
| 973 |
| 972 |
| 971 |
| 970 |
| 947 |
| 946 |
| 900 |
| 608 |
| 606 |
| 3824 |
| 3341 |
| 3340 |

14

| 3825 |
| 722 |
| 721 |
| 720 |
| 922 |
| 921 |
| 920 |
| 919 |
| 918 |
| 3770 |
| 951 |
| 945 |
| 3856 |
| 402 |
| 3776 |
| 301 |
| 400 |
| 300 |
| 3855 |
| 3854 |
| 3853 |
| 3827 |
| 977 |
| 976 |
| 3826 |
| 975 |

15

| 948 |
| 754 |
| 758 |
| 3778 |
| 356 |
| 3830 |
| 355 |
| 3777 |
| 3779 |
| 3859 |
| 3858 |
| 3857 |
| 3774 |
| 950 |
| 3773 |
| 3064 |
| 407 |
| 3772 |
| 632 |
| 453 |
| 452 |
| 451 |
| 3861 |
| 3860 |

16

| 712 |
| 739 |
| 738 |
| 437 |
| 436 |
| 435 |
| 434 |
| 433 |
| 801 |
| 898 |
| 938 |
| 3371 |
| 543 |
| 3864 |
| 3863 |
| 3862 |
| 842 |
| 841 |
| 840 |
| 839 |
| 838 |
| 3790 |
| 3781 |
| 3031 |

Exclusive numbering system of DMC © 2002

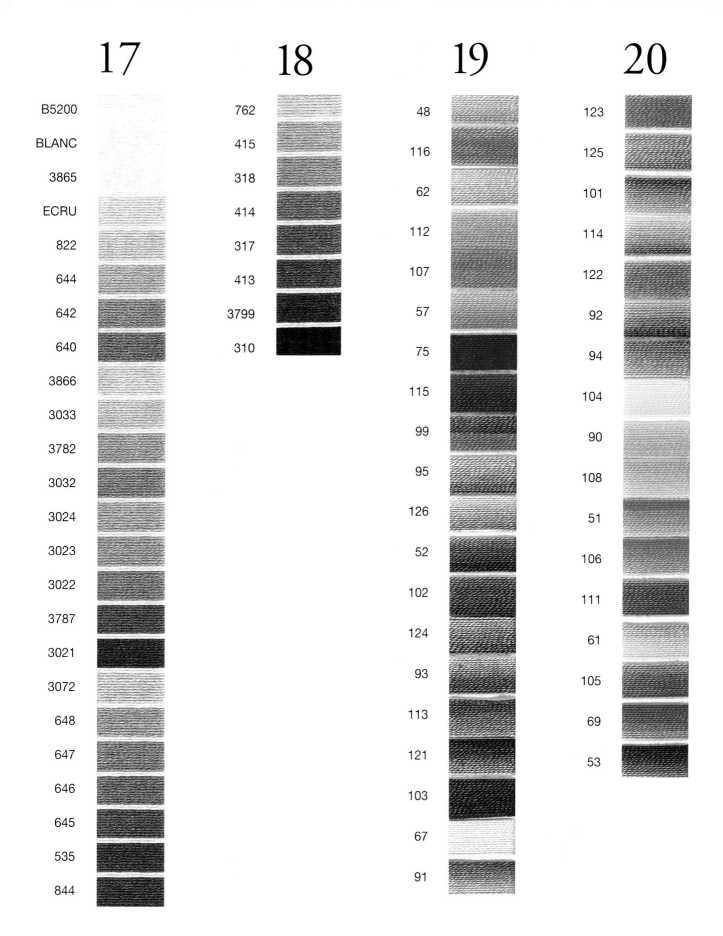

17

B5200
BLANC
3865
ECRU
822
644
642
640
3866
3033
3782
3032
3024
3023
3022
3787
3021
3072
648
647
646
645
535
844

18

762
415
318
414
317
413
3799
310

19

48
116
62
112
107
57
75
115
99
95
126
52
102
124
93
113
121
103
67
91

20

123
125
101
114
122
92
94
104
90
108
51
106
111
61
105
69
53

Anchor conversion chart

This conversion chart should only be used a guide as it is not always possible to provide exact substitutes.

An * indicates that the Anchor shade has been used more than once and additional care should be taken to avoid duplication within a design.

Some Anchor shades do not appear on this chart as they are unique to the Anchor range.

DMC	Anchor	DMC	Anchor	DMC	Anchor	DMC	Anchor	DMC	Anchor	DMC	Anchor	DMC	Anchor
B5200	1	444	291	700	228	819	271	943	189	3346	267*	3808	1068
White	2	445	28	701	227	820	134	945	881	3347	266*	3809	1066*
Ecru	110*	451	233	702	226	822	390	946	332	3348	264	3810	1066*
208	109	452	232	703	238	823	152*	947	330*	3350	77	3811	1060
210	108	453	231	704	256*	824	164	948	1011	3354	74	3812	188
211	342	469	267*	712	926	825	162*	950	4146	3362	263	3813	875*
221	897*	470	266*	718	88	826	161*	951	1010	3363	262	3814	1074
223	895	471	265	720	326	827	160	954	203*	3364	261	3815	877*
224	893	472	253	721	324	828	9159	955	203*	3371	896	3816	876*
225	1026	498	1005	722	323*	829	906	956	40*	3607	87	3817	875*
300	352	500	683	725	305	830	277*	957	50	3608	86	3818	923*
301	1049*	501	878	726	295*	831	277*	958	187	3609	85	3819	278
304	19	502	877*	727	293	832	907	959	186	3685	1028	3820	306
307	289	503	876*	729	890	833	874*	961	76*	3687	68	3821	305*
309	42	504	206*	730	845*	834	874*	962	75*	3688	75*	3822	295*
310	403	517	1628	731	281*	838	1088	963	872	3689	49	3823	386
311	148	518	1039	732	281*	839	1086	964	185	3705	35*	3824	8*
312	979	519	1038	733	280	840	1084	966	240	3706	35*	3825	323*
315	1019*	520	862*	734	279	841	1082	970	925	3708	31	3826	1049*
316	1017	522	860	738	361*	842	1080	971	316*	3712	1023	3827	311
317	400	523	859	739	366	844	1041	972	298	3713	1020	3829	901*
318	235*	524	858	740	316*	869	375	973	290	3716	25	3830	5975
319	1044*	535	401	741	304	890	218	975	357	3721	896	48	1207
320	215	543	933	742	303	891	35*	976	1001	3722	1027	51	1220*
321	47	550	101*	743	302	892	33*	977	1002	3726	1018	52	1209*
322	978	552	99	744	301	893	27	986	246	3727	1016	57	1203*
326	598	553	98	745	300	894	26	987	244	3731	76*	61	1218*
327	1018	554	95	746	275	895	1044*	988	243	3733	75*	62	1201*
333	119	561	212	747	158	898	380	989	242	3740	872	67	1212
334	977	562	210	754	1012	899	38	991	1076	3743	869	69	1218*
335	40*	563	208	758	9575	900	333	992	1072	3746	1030	75	1206*
336	150	564	206*	760	1022	902	897*	993	1070	3747	120	90	1217*
340	118	580	924	761	1021	904	258	995	410	3750	1036	91	1211
341	117	581	281*	762	234	905	257	996	433	3752	1032	92	1215*
347	1025	597	1064	772	259	906	256*	3011	856	3753	1031	93	1210*
349	13*	598	1062	775	128	907	255	3012	855	3755	140	94	1216
350	11	600	59*	776	24	909	923*	3013	853	3756	1037	95	1209*
351	10	601	63*	778	968	910	230	3021	905*	3760	162*	99	1204
352	9	602	57	780	309	911	205	3022	8581*	3761	928	101	1213*
353	8*	603	62*	781	308*	912	209	3023	899	3765	170	102	1209*
355	1014	604	55	782	308*	913	204	3024	388*	3766	167	103	1210*
356	1013*	605	1094	783	307	915	1029	3031	905*	3768	779	104	1217*
367	216	606	334	791	178	917	89	3032	898*	3770	1009	105	1218*
368	214	608	330*	792	941	918	341	3033	387*	3772	1007	106	1203*
369	1043	610	889	793	176	919	340	3041	871	3773	1008	107	1203*
370	888*	611	898*	794	175	920	1004	3042	870	3774	778	108	1220*
371	887*	612	832	796	133	921	1003*	3045	888*	3776	1048	111	1218*
372	887*	613	831	797	132	922	1003*	3046	887*	3777	1015	112	1201*
400	351	632	936	798	146	924	851	3047	852	3778	1013*	113	1210*
402	1047	640	393	799	145	926	850	3051	845*	3779	868	114	1215*
407	914	642	392	800	144	927	849	3052	844	3781	1050	115	1206*
413	2368	644	391	801	359	928	274	3053	843	3782	388*	121	1210*
414	235*	645	273	806	169	930	1035	3064	883	3787	904*	122	1215*
415	398	646	8581*	807	168	931	1034	3072	397	3790	904*	124	1210*
420	374	647	1040	809	130	932	1033	3078	292	3799	236*	125	1213*
422	372	648	900	813	161*	934	862*	3325	129	3801	1098	126	1209*
433	358	666	46	814	45	935	861	3326	36	3802	1019*		
434	310	676	891	815	44	936	846	3328	1024	3803	69		
435	365	677	361*	816	43	937	268*	3340	329	3804	63*		
436	363	680	901*	817	13*	938	381	3341	328	3806	62*		
437	362	699	923*	818	23*	939	152*	3345	268*	3807	122		

Suppliers

Most large department stores carry a good range of fabrics, threads and accessories. Look in the Yellow Pages under Art & Craft Equipment or Needlecraft Retailers.

UK

DMC Creative World Ltd
Pullman Road, Wigston
Leicestershire
LE18 2DY
Tel: (0116) 281 1040
www.dmc.com
DMC threads can be found in branches of John Lewis nationwide. Phone for your nearest stockist.

Craft Creations
Ingersoll House
Delamare Road
Cheshunt
Herts EN8 9HD
Tel: (01992) 781 900
www.craftcreations.com
Card blanks, tassels, etc. Mail order only

David Morgan Ltd
26 The Hayes
Cardiff
CF1 1UG
Tel: (029) 2022 1011

Delicate Stitches
339 Kentish Town Road
London NW5 2TJ
Tel: (020) 7267 9403

The Embroidery Shop
51 William Street
Edinburgh EH3 7LW
Tel: (0131) 225 8642
Fax: (0131) 663 8255
E-mail:
embroideryshop@gofornet.co.uk

Framecraft Miniatures Ltd.
Lichfield Road, Brownhills
Walsall, West Midlands
WS8 6LH
Tel: (01543) 360 842
www.framecraft.com
Special boxes etc. for embroidery. Mail order and stockists.

Stitches
355 Warwick Road
Olton, Solihull
B91 1BQ
Tel: (0121) 706 1048

Sussex Needlecraft
37 Warwick Street
Worthing
BN11 3DQ
Tel: (01903) 823655

Willow Fabrics
95 Town Lane
Mobberley
Cheshire
WA16 7HH
Tel: (0800) 056 7811
www.willowfabrics.com
Embroidery fabrics. Mail order only.

SOUTH AFRICA

Cape Town Sewing Centre
78 Darling Street
Cape Town
Tel: (021) 465 2111

Johannesburg Sewing Centre
109 Pritchard Street
Johannesburg
Gauteng
Tel: (011) 333 3060

Sew & Save
Mimosa Mall
131 Brandwag
Bloemfontein
Tel: (051) 444 3122

Stitch Craft Centre
5 Umhlanga Centre
Ridge Road
Umhlanga Rocks
Durban
Tel: (031) 561 5822

Stitch Talk
Centurion Park
Centurion Square
Pretoria
Tel: (012) 663 2035

Thimbles & Threads
6 Quarry Centre
Hilton
Pietermaritzburg
Tel: (033) 43 1966

AUSTRALIA

Barbour Threads Pty Ltd
Suite E3
2 Cowpasture Place
Wetherill Park
NSW 2164
Tel: (02) 9756 5466
Freecall: (1800) 337 929

Birch Haberdashery and Craft
EC Birch Pty Ltd
Richmond
Victoria 3121
Tel: (03) 9429 4944

DMC Needlecraft Pty Ltd
51-55 Carrington Road
Marrickville
NSW 2204
Tel: (02) 9559 3088

Sewing Thread Specialists
41-43 Day Street (North)
Silverwater
NSW 2128
Tel: (1300) 65 3855

Sullivans Haberdashery and Craft Wholesalers
40 Parramatta Road
Underwood
Queensland 4119
Tel: (07) 3209 4799

NEW ZEALAND

The Embroiderer
140 Hinemoa Street
Birkenhead
Auckland
Tel: (09) 419 0900

Nancy's Embroidery
273 Tinakori Road
Thorndon
Wellington
Tel: (04) 473 4047

Spotlight Stores
Carry a very large range of fabrics and haberdashery materials
Manukau - Tel: (09) 263 6760
or 0800 162 373
Wairau Park - Tel: (09) 444 0220
or 0800 224 123
Hamilton - Tel: (07) 839 1793
New Plymouth - Tel: (06) 757 3575
Wellington - Tel: (04) 472 5600
Christchurch - Tel: (03) 377 6121

Stitches
351 Colombo Street
Sydenham
Christchurch
Tel: (03) 379 1868
Email: stitches@xtra.co.nz

For a wider listing of embroidery suppliers nationwide, consult your Yellow Pages under 'Handcrafts & Supplies' or search under 'Shopping: Hobbies & Games: Handcrafts' on www.yellowpages.co.nz

Index

address book, architectural drawing, 59
Aida fabric, 8
Anchor conversion chart, 110
animal motifs, 64–85
apron pad, cow, 69
architectural drawing, 56–9
Art Deco rose sewing set, 18–21

baby set, teddy bear, 74–7
back stitch, 11
bathrooms: seaside, 82–5
　Turkish, 100–3
bed linen: blue bird, 78–81
　camellia, 34–7
　playing card motifs, 95
bib, teddy bear baby set, 77
bird motifs, blue bird bed linen, 78–81
blanket patch, teddy bear baby set, 77
blue and white sampler, 88–91
blue bird bed linen, 78–81
bowls: blue and white sampler, 91
　Japanese lady, 63
　blue and white sampler, 91
boxes: blue bird motif, 81
　camellia motif, 37
breakfast set, cute cats, 70–3

camellia bed linen, 34–7
cats breakfast set, 70–3
charts, 9
chenille needles, 9
coasters: cute cats breakfast set, 73
　green leaves table linen, 29
cockerel oven pad, 69
colour charts, 104–10
cotton, stranded, 8
cow apron patch, 69
cushions: playing card motifs, 94
　red poppies, 25
cute cats breakfast set, 70–3

daisy picnic basket, 30–3

edges, preventing fraying, 10
embroidery hoops and frames, 10
equipment, 8–10
evenweave linen, 8

fabrics, 8
farmyard animals, 66–9
flower motifs: Art Deco rose sewing set,
　18–21

camellia bed linen, 34–7
　daisy picnic basket, 30–3
　red poppies, 22–5
frames, embroidery, 10
French knots, 11
fridge magnet, windmill motif, 47
fruit motifs, 14–17

geometric motifs, 86–103
gingham playmat and pram toys, 52–5
green leaves table linen, 26–9
green linen teaset, 48–51
guest towels: seashell bathroom, 43
　Turkish bathroom, 103

half cross stitch, 11
hardanger fabric, 8
hoops, embroidery, 10

jam pot cover, summer fruits, 17
Japanese lady, 60–3
jewellery box, blue bird motif, 81

leaf motifs, green leaves table linen, 26–9
linen, evenweave, 8

magnet, windmill motif, 47
materials, 8
mug, cute cats breakfast set, 73

napkins: green leaves table linen, 29
　green linen teaset, 51
　red and white table linen, 99
napkin rings: green linen teaset, 51
　red and white table linen, 99
needle case, Art Deco rose, 20
needles, 8–9
notebooks: blue and white sampler, 91
　playing card motifs, 95

oven pad, cockerel, 69

patchwork play mat, 54
picnic basket, daisy, 30–3
picture motifs, 38–63
pictures: architectural drawing, 59
　Japanese lady, 62–3
　red poppies, 24
　seashell bathroom, 43
pillow cases: blue bird bed linen, 81
　camellia bed linen, 37
pin cushion, Art Deco rose, 20

placemat, cute cats breakfast set, 72–3
play mat, patchwork, 54
playing card motifs, 92–5
poppy motif, 22–5
pram toys, gingham, 55
pressing work, 10

quarter cross.stitch, 11

red and white table linen, 96–9
red poppies, 22–5
rose sewing set, Art Deco, 18–21
runner, red and white table linen, 98

sampler, blue and white, 88–91
scissor fob, Art Deco rose, 20
scissors, 10
seashell bathroom, 40–3
seaside bathroom, 82–5
sewing set, Art Deco rose, 18–21
sheet bands: blue bird bed linen, 80
　camellia bed linen, 36
　playing card motifs, 95
shelf edging, windmill motif, 47
soap bag, Turkish bathroom, 103
stitches, 10–11
stranded cotton, 8
summer fruits, 14–17

table cloths: daisy picnic cloth, 33
　green leaves table linen, 29
table runner, red and white table linen, 98
tapestry needles, 8
tea towels: summer fruits, 17
　windmill motif, 46
teddy bear baby set, 74–7
threads, 8
　Anchor conversion chart, 110
　DMC chart, 104–9
three-quarters cross stitch, 11
towels: farmyard animals, 68
　seashell bathroom, 43
　seaside motifs, 84
　Turkish bathroom, 103
tray cloth, green linen teaset, 51
trinket box, camellia motif, 37
Turkish bathroom, 100–3

wall hanging, blue and white sampler, 91
washing, 10
windmill pantry, 44–7